First World War
and Army of Occupation
War Diary
France, Belgium and Germany

31 DIVISION
Divisional Troops
210 Field Company Royal Engineers
8 March 1916 - 30 April 1919

WO95/2352/1

The Naval & Military Press Ltd
www.nmarchive.com
Published in association with The National Archives

Published by

The Naval & Military Press Ltd

Unit 10 Ridgewood Industrial Park,

Uckfield, East Sussex,

TN22 5QE England

Tel: +44 (0) 1825 749494

www.naval-military-press.com

www.nmarchive.com

This diary has been reprinted in facsimile from the original. Any imperfections are inevitably reproduced and the quality may fall short of modern type and cartographic standards.

© **Crown Copyright**
Images reproduced by permission of The National Archives, London, England, 2015.

Contents

Document type	Place/Title	Date From	Date To
Heading	WO95/2352/1		
Heading	31st Division Divl Engineers 210th Field Coy R.E. Mar 1916-Mar 1919		
War Diary	Marseilles	08/03/1916	08/03/1916
War Diary	Pont Remy	10/03/1916	10/03/1916
War Diary	Court	11/03/1916	31/03/1916
Heading	War Diary Of Edward Happer April 1916. 31 April 210. F.C.R.E. Vol. 2		
War Diary	Bus	01/04/1916	30/04/1916
War Diary	Bus & Courcelles	01/05/1916	31/05/1916
War Diary	Bus-Les Artois	01/06/1916	29/06/1916
War Diary	Bus-Les Artois	01/06/1916	30/06/1916
Heading	War Diary Of 210th Field Company R.E. From July 1st To July 31st 1916 Volume VII.		
War Diary	Bus Les Artois	01/07/1916	04/07/1916
War Diary	Beauval	05/07/1916	05/07/1916
War Diary	Bernaville	06/07/1916	09/07/1916
War Diary	Robecq	10/07/1916	14/07/1916
War Diary	Bout-Deville	15/07/1916	31/07/1916
Heading	War Diary Of 210th Field Company R.E. From August 1st To August 31st 1916. Vol 6		
War Diary Miscellaneous	R.36a.6.8	01/08/1916	31/08/1916
Heading	War Diary 210 Field Coy R.E. 31st Division September 1916. Vol 7		
War Diary	R.36.a.6.8	01/09/1916	16/09/1916
War Diary	R.36.a.6.8	01/09/1916	17/09/1916
War Diary	Gorre	18/09/1916	30/09/1916
Heading	War Diary of Edward Happer-Major R.E. 210th Fld Co R.E. From October 1st 1916 To October 31st 1916. Volume. 10		
War Diary	Givenchy	01/10/1916	05/10/1916
War Diary	Busnes	08/10/1916	08/10/1916
War Diary	Doullens	09/10/1916	09/10/1916
War Diary	Thievres	12/10/1916	13/10/1916
War Diary	Coigneux	14/10/1916	16/10/1916
War Diary	Hebuterne	17/10/1916	17/10/1916
War Diary	Coigneux	17/10/1916	31/10/1916
Heading	War Diary Of Edward Happer Major R.E. Volume 9 From 1st November 1916 To 30 November 1916. 210 Fd Coy.		
War Diary	Coigneux	01/11/1916	30/11/1916
Heading	War Diary Of A.B. Clough Major R.E. From 1st December 1916 To 31st December 1916. 210 Fd Coy. Vol 10		
War Diary	Coigneux	01/12/1916	31/12/1916
War Diary	War Diary 210th Field Company R.E. 31st Division. January 1917. Vol XI.		
War Diary	Coigneux	01/12/1916	08/12/1916
War Diary	Occoches	09/12/1916	15/12/1916

War Diary	Gezaincourt	16/12/1916	31/12/1916
Heading	War Diary 210th Field Coy R.E. 31st Division February 1917. Vol 12		
War Diary	Beaussart	01/02/1917	04/02/1917
War Diary	Bernaville	05/02/1917	18/02/1917
War Diary	Beauval	19/02/1917	19/02/1917
War Diary	Coigneux	21/02/1917	28/02/1917
Heading	War Diary. 210th Field Company R.E. 31st Division March 1917. Vol 13		
War Diary	Coigneux	01/03/1917	08/03/1917
War Diary	Colincamps	09/03/1917	18/03/1917
War Diary	Beauval	19/03/1917	19/03/1917
War Diary	Vacquerie	20/03/1917	20/03/1917
War Diary	Gauchin	21/03/1917	21/03/1917
War Diary	Cauchy	22/03/1917	23/03/1917
War Diary	Bourecq	24/03/1917	24/03/1917
War Diary	St. Venant	25/03/1917	31/03/1917
Heading	War Diary. 210th Field Coy R.E. 31st Division April 1917. Vol 14		
War Diary	St Venant	01/04/1917	07/04/1917
War Diary	Gonnehem	08/04/1917	10/04/1917
War Diary	Bruay	11/04/1917	11/04/1917
War Diary	Barlin	12/04/1917	12/04/1917
War Diary	Villers Brulin	14/04/1917	16/04/1917
War Diary	Ecoivres	17/04/1917	17/04/1917
War Diary	Roclincourt	18/04/1917	30/04/1917
Heading	War Diary. 210th Field Coy. R.E. 31st Division May 1917. Volume XVII.		
War Diary	Roclincourt	01/05/1917	31/05/1917
Heading	War Diary. 210th Field Company R.E. June 1917. Volume XVIII.		
War Diary	Rollincourt	01/06/1917	30/06/1917
Heading	War Diary Of 210th Field Company. R.E. From July 1st. 1917 To July 31st. 1917. Volume XIX.		
War Diary	Roclincourt	01/07/1917	03/07/1917
War Diary	Ecoivres	04/07/1917	12/07/1917
War Diary	Au Rietz (A.14.a.3.9.)	13/07/1917	31/07/1917
Heading	War Diary Of 210th Field Company. R.E. From 1/8/17 To 31/8/17. Volume XX.		
War Diary	Aux Rietz	01/08/1917	31/08/1917
Heading	War Diary. 210th Field Company. R.E. 31st Division September 1917. Volume XXI.		
War Diary	Aux Reitz	01/09/1917	04/09/1917
War Diary	6th Onwards Ecurie	05/09/1917	30/09/1917
Heading	War Diary 210 Field Coy. R.E. 31st Division October 1917. Volume XX.		
War Diary	Ecurie	01/10/1917	31/10/1917
Heading	Confidential. War Diary Of 210th Field Company. R.E. 1/11/17 To 30/11/17 Volume XXI.		
War Diary	Ecurie.	01/11/1917	30/11/1917
Heading	War Diary Of 210th Field Company. R.E. From 1/12/17 To 31/12/17. Volume XXII.		
War Diary	Ecurie	01/12/1917	06/12/1917
War Diary	St. Catherine. (Arras).	07/12/1917	20/12/1917
War Diary	Ecurie	21/12/1917	31/12/1917

Heading	War Diary Of 210th Field Company. R.E. 1/1/18 To 31/1/18. Volume XXV.		
War Diary	Ecurie	01/01/1918	31/01/1918
Heading	War Diary Of 210th Field Company. R.E. From 1/2/18 To 28/2/18. Volume XXVI.		
War Diary	Ecurie	01/02/1918	28/02/1918
Heading	31st Divisional Engineers War Diary 210th Field Company R.E. March 1918		
Heading	War Diary. Of 210th Field Company. R.E. From 1/3/18 To 31/3/18. Volume XXV		
War Diary	Ecurie	01/03/1918	22/03/1918
War Diary	Blairville	23/03/1918	24/03/1918
War Diary	Courcelles	24/03/1918	25/03/1918
War Diary	Monchy.	25/03/1918	31/03/1918
Heading	31st Divisional Engineers 210th Field Company R.E. April 1918		
Heading	War Diary Of 210th Field Company. R.E. From 1/4/18 To 30/4/18. Volume XXVIII		
War Diary	Souastre	01/04/1918	01/04/1918
War Diary	Warluzel	02/04/1918	03/04/1918
War Diary	Caucort	03/04/1918	06/04/1918
War Diary	Hermin	08/04/1918	09/04/1918
War Diary	Wanquetin	09/04/1918	10/04/1918
War Diary	Tinques	10/04/1918	11/04/1918
War Diary	Strazeele	12/04/1918	14/04/1918
War Diary	Borre	15/04/1918	27/04/1918
War Diary	Hondeghem	28/04/1918	30/04/1918
Heading	War Diary Of 210th Field Company. R.E. From 1/5/18 To 31/5/18. Volume XXIX.		
War Diary	Hondeghem	01/05/1918	31/05/1918
Heading	War Diary Of 210th Field Company. R.E. From June 1st, 1918 To June 30th, 1918. Volume XXX.		
War Diary	Blaringhem	01/06/1918	14/06/1918
War Diary	Staples	15/06/1918	16/06/1918
War Diary	Racquinghem	17/06/1918	20/06/1918
War Diary	Hazebrouck	20/06/1918	30/06/1918
Heading	War Diary Of 210th Field Company. R.E. From 1/7/18 To 31/7/18. Volume XXXI.		
War Diary	Au Souverain	01/07/1918	31/07/1918
Heading	War Diary Of 210th Field Company. R.E. From 1/8/18 To 31/8/18. Volume XXXII.		
War Diary	Au Souverain	01/08/1918	11/08/1918
War Diary	Gd Hassard	11/08/1918	22/08/1918
War Diary	Le Peuplier	23/08/1918	30/08/1918
War Diary	Fletre	31/08/1918	31/08/1918
Heading	War Diary Of 210th Field Company. R.E. From 1st Sept. To 30th Sept. 1918. Volume XXXI.		
War Diary	Balleul	01/09/1918	11/09/1918
War Diary	Caestre	13/09/1918	30/09/1918
Heading	War Diary Of 210th Field Company. R.E. From 1/10/18 To 31/10/18. Volume XXXIV.		
War Diary	Ploegsteert	01/10/1918	16/10/1918
War Diary	Warneton	16/10/1918	17/10/1918
War Diary	Croix Blanche.	18/10/1918	18/10/1918
War Diary	Turcoing	19/10/1918	21/10/1918
War Diary	Leers Nord	22/10/1918	23/10/1918

War Diary	Mouscron	25/10/1918	26/10/1918
War Diary	Staceghem	27/10/1918	30/10/1918
War Diary	Vichte	30/10/1918	31/10/1918
Heading	War Diary Of 210th Field Company. R.E. From 1/11/18 To 30/11/18. Volume XXXV.		
War Diary	Vichte	01/11/1918	02/11/1918
War Diary	Halluin	03/11/1918	05/11/1918
War Diary	Courtrai	06/11/1918	08/11/1918
War Diary	Ooteghem	08/11/1918	09/11/1918
War Diary	Orrior	10/11/1918	10/11/1918
War Diary	Renaix	11/11/1918	12/11/1918
War Diary	Avelghem	14/11/1918	14/11/1918
War Diary	Lauwe	15/11/1918	23/11/1918
War Diary	Menin	24/11/1918	24/11/1918
War Diary	Ypres	25/11/1918	25/11/1918
War Diary	Steenvorde	26/11/1918	26/11/1918
War Diary	Staples	27/11/1918	27/11/1918
War Diary	Ludausques	28/11/1918	30/11/1918
Heading	War Diary Of 210th Field Company. R.E. From 1/12/18 To 31/12/18. Volume XXXIV.		
War Diary	Zudausques	01/12/1918	01/12/1918
War Diary	St. Omer	02/12/1918	31/12/1918
Heading	War Diary Of The 210th. Field Company R.E. For The Month Of January. 1919. Volume 37		
War Diary	St. Omer	01/01/1919	31/01/1919
Heading	War Diary. 210th Field Company, Royal Engineers, February, 1919. Vol 36		
War Diary	St. Omer.	01/02/1919	28/02/1919
War Diary	St. Omer	01/03/1919	31/03/1919
War Diary	St. Omer.	06/03/1919	30/04/1919

31ST DIVISION
DIVL ENGINEERS

210TH FIELD COY. R.E.
MAR 1916-MAR 1919

31ST DIVISION
DIVL ENGINEERS

Army Form C. 2118.

WAR DIARY
or
INTELLIGENCE SUMMARY. MARCH 1916 2/10. Field Co. R.E.
(Erase heading not required.)

Instructions regarding War Diaries and Intelligence Summaries are contained in F. S. Regs., Part II. and the Staff Manual respectively. Title pages will be prepared in manuscript.

Place	Date	Hour	Summary of Events and Information	Remarks and references to Appendices
Marseilles	8/3/16		Entrained at Marseille at 4.30 p.m. Leaving at 7.36 p.m.	
Pont Remy	10/3/16		Arrived Pont Remy. 6 p.m. En Camp hut for night.	
Pont Remy cont	11/3/16		Marched from Pont Remy 5 mile const. men billets at working Con's	
"	12 "		Same day	
"	14/3/16		Whole Company engaged in clearing out billets. Receiving clothes Latrine line - lime etc.	
"	14 "		Getting equipment. Camped. advance store by other	
"	26/3/16		Marched from Pont Remy cont to Longpre	
"	27/3/16		" " Longpre " Lucel	
"	28/3/16 to 3/16		" " Flexecourt " Beauval	
"	29 3/16		" " Beauval	
"	30 3/16		" " Beauval " Bus - les - Artois	
"	31/3/16		Arranging & cleaning up & setting down at Camp Bules - Artois	

31 April
210.Y.P.RE
vol 2

Confidential

Note during of
Edward Stopper
April 1916

WAR DIARY / INTELLIGENCE SUMMARY

Army Form C. 2118.

Place	Date	Hour	Summary of Events and Information	Remarks and references to Appendices
Bus	1/4/16 to 30/4/16		One section of Coy Engineers (No 4) moved to Busseboom - rest of Coy working at R.E. Park and new huts at half moon, mostly the Nissen type. One section of the Company (under 2nd Lieut .....) moved to Brandhoek and worked on Rest Line under orders of O.C. 223rd Coy R.E. until 21st April, this section then returned to Bus. Two sections of the Company (No 1 & 3) remained at Bus and were engaged on following work - metalling of trek after 34th Section of Wells at Bus, dead horse removal road - construction of light rly from Bus and to General R.E. Park. No 4 Section returned to the Company. Part of Dwarfield Voisin Huts also engaged in clearing up trenches in Rein area, obtaining & distributing equipment, vehicles, clothing & fitting — to the Canadian Defence subsidy Panels on the connecting defences including trenches, dugouts communications. Mounted section engaged in transport & conveying in orders not &c.	

[Signature]
COMMANDING
210TH FIELD COMPANY R.E.

210 FERE
Vol 3

Army Form C. 2118.

WAR DIARY
or
INTELLIGENCE SUMMARY.

(Erase heading not required.)

31

Place	Date	Hour	Summary of Events and Information	Remarks and references to Appendices
Bus & Couscelles	1916 May 1st to May 31		One Section of the Company working R.E. Park and workshops Couscelles. One Section of the Company engaged on the erection of 96 huts (for accommodation of troops) 20 of which were hutted. Officers Mess hut & Picture. 4 R.A.M.C huts. One Section working on front line with 94th Infantry Brigade from 18/5/16. Ration dumps. G.O.C's dug out. bomb stores. Trench signs. Winch construction. revetting and trench digging. The remainder of the Company engaged in the following works:— Emir Bus water supply — laying 4" pipe line 1½ mile — construction and erection of wooden tank (9000 galls.) & another construction and concrete (1000 galls.). Staging for and erection of reservoir and tanks (1000 galls.): Staging for and erection of tanks. Water troughs and connections throughout. Installation of 4 bins in well at Bus and linking continued. Erection of staging and tank connections as well. Throughout Wood. Construction of three communication trenches N.W. of Mailly Cemetery Grove Road of Cheerok Avenue.	JS

WAR DIARY

INTELLIGENCE SUMMARY.

Army Form C. 2118.

Place	Date	Hour	Summary of Events and Information	Remarks and references to Appendices
Bus to Crucelles	1916 May 1st to May 31st	6.05	S.E. corner of Crecent Trench to Watling Street. K32 20 to Delauney Avenue. Erection of shelters for bomb store Bus – Bad weather & stores at B.H.Q. Bus – Bad erection of lectern room & Officers quarters. Advanced School Bus. Construction of dug-out for large motor lorry Crucelles. Heavy flies knocking packet. Adjournee RE work proper allotted to this company.	

J Clapp Hayne RE
O.C. 20th v. F.C.R.

WAR DIARY

Army Form C. 2118.

June

XXX / 210 J R E

Vol 4

Place	Date	Hour	Summary of Events and Information	Remarks and references to Appendices
BUS-LES ARTOIS	JUNE 1ST — 29TH		Front line area work (2 sections) Note:- On the 13th inst. 12 Sappers from 3 + 4 Sections + on the 15th inst. 4 Sappers from 3 + 4 Sections to the Seaforth to help Nos. 1 + 2 Sections. (1). Constructed 4 (four) ration, ammunition + water dumps. " 17 (seventeen) Artillery bridges - placed 10 (ten) (2). " in position + carried remainder to suitable dumps for replacement of destroyed bridges. (3). Formed R.E. dump in observation wood. (4). Constructed 8 (Eight) bomb shorts in Secewa trench. (5). " 6 (six) Artillery O.P.s. (6). " 2 (two) Brigade O.P.s (7). " 35 (thirty five) feet of Russian Sap. total length 20 (seventy) feet. Note:- A large proportion of the time occupied in this work was taken up in clearing out and out after bombardment (8). Commenced 4 (four) deep dug outs - reached an average depth of 20 (twenty) feet.	

Army Form C. 2118.

WAR DIARY
or
INTELLIGENCE SUMMARY.

(Erase heading not required.)

Instructions regarding War Diaries and Intelligence Summaries are contained in F.S. Regs., Part II. and the Staff Manual respectively. Title pages will be prepared in manuscript.

Place	Date	Hour	Summary of Events and Information	Remarks and references to Appendices
BUS-LES ATOIS	JUNE 1ST TO 29TH		(9) - Supplied R.E. supervision clearing and opening out 8 (eight) Assembly trenches and 4 (four) communication trenches.	
			(10) - Construction of small emplacements (4) - Supplied R.E. Supervision for erection of same in front line.	
			(11). Construction of one advanced slit (24) in front line area.	
			(12). Two plumbers repairing and supervising water supply in front area.	
			(13). Constructed Sotia entrance to B.H.Q. dugout in DUNMOW.	
			(14) Construction of "Signals" dugout in LE CATEAU gallery completed. Further work stopped as working parties could not be spared.	
			(15) Supervised cutting & removal of barbed wire in front of ROB ROY, MONK & CAMPION.	
			(16) General supervision and R.E. assistance in ordinary trench maintenance, in area allotted to 210th Field Company.	

Army Form C. 2118.

WAR DIARY
or
INTELLIGENCE SUMMARY.
(Erase heading not required.)

Place	Date	Hour	Summary of Events and Information	Remarks and references to Appendices
BUS-LES ARTOIS	JUNE 1ST TO 29TH		17- Improved deepened and revetted PYLON AV. and PALESTINE (yellowline) Backwork - 2 sections (less 2 1 (horses, one) sappers) detailed for front line area) and mounted section. 1- Wells at BUS-LES-ARTOIS:- Erection of 2 (two) engines & pumps- 3 (three) tanks and 4 (four) stand pipes. Sinking of wells continued - depth of each well 130 (one hundred and thirty) feet. 2. Wells at WARNIMONT: Improvements and repairs, wire fencing &c. 3. COUIN-BUS water supply. Construction of reservoir at BUS-LES-ARTOIS (new wooden water tank) 20'x 18'x 6'- Laying 4" (four inch) pipe line from this reservoir to 4TH Division watering area. Erection of troughs fittings and connections, handed over for 4th Division water supply Extensions, improvement & repairs to 31st Divisional supply 4. Completion of following works in progress in last months Summary	

WAR DIARY or INTELLIGENCE SUMMARY

Army Form C. 2118.

Place	Date	Hour	Summary of Events and Information	Remarks and references to Appendices
BUS-LES-ARTOIS	JUNE 1ST TO 29TH		Lecture room and Officer quarters divisional School Bus-Les-Artois. Dug out for motor lorry (COURCELLES). 5. Felling trees, cutting same into suitable lengths, making pickets &c. 6. MOUNTED SECTION - Transport for all above work. 7. General R.E. work in area allotted to this Company.	
	JUNE 30TH		Three sections (1, 2 & 3) in trenches (forward area) acting in accordance with CREs orders & Battle orders. Supervision & repair of bridges - water supplies (mains and tanks) general repair work. One Section (4) in BUS-LES-ARTOIS Supervising water supply - pumping engines &c. Mounted Section in BUS-LES-ARTOIS - Transport &c.	

Clofforthay? RE
O.C. 110 Fa. Ja RE

Confidential

War Diary

of

210th Field Company. R.E.

From July 1st to July 31st 1916

Volume VII

Army Form C. 2118.

WAR DIARY
or
INTELLIGENCE SUMMARY.
(Erase heading not required.)

Instructions regarding War Diaries and Intelligence Summaries are contained in F. S. Regs., Part II. and the Staff Manual respectively. Title pages will be prepared in manuscript.

Place	Date	Hour	Summary of Events and Information	Remarks and references to Appendices
Bus les Artois	July 1st & 2nd		Nos 1, 2 & 3 Sections in SAPPER TRENCH - No 4 Section in BUS-LES-ARTOIS - superintending cable supply - Tanks - general work here - Mounted section - general transport	
	3rd		Nos 1 & 3 Section in COURCELLES - Nos 2 & 4 and mounted Sections in BUS-LES-ARTOIS.	
	4th		Nos 1 & 3 Sections move into BUS-LES-ARTOIS.	
BEAUVAL 5th BERNAVILLE 6th	5th to 7th.		Whole company marched from BUS-LES-ARTOIS to BEAUVAL. BEAUVAL to BERNAVILLE	
	8.		Whole company in BERNAVILLE	
	9th.		Whole company marched nd of BERNAVILLE 11.45 P.M to AUX-LES-CHATEAUX and entrained here for THIENNES	
ROBECQ	10th		Arrived THIENNES detrained there and marched to ROBECQ	
	5th 14.		In ROBECQ - infantry training - temporary huts	

2353 Wt. W2544/1454 700,000 5/15 D. D. & L. A.D.S.S./Forms/C. 2118

Army Form C. 2118.

WAR DIARY
or
INTELLIGENCE SUMMARY.
(Erase heading not required.)

Place	Date	Hour	Summary of Events and Information	Remarks and references to Appendices
BOUT-DE-VILLE	July 15		Whole Company marched to BOUT-DE-VILLE	
	16		In BOUT-DE-VILLE - improv billets & arrangements for accommodation given.	
	19			
	20			
	21st		Whole Company marched to Sheet 36A Edition 6. Scale 1: 40000 R 36.a.6.8. x cleared out billets (badly required) erected huts. horse lines &c.	
	22nd			
	23rd			
	to			
	31st		One section engaged in work in line. revetment & cleaning out of trenches. Sand bagging. laying trench boards. Constructing revetment frames. dug outs &c. making panels & placing of sign posts & &c.	

(signed) .... R.E.
COMMANDING
210th FIELD COMPANY R.E.

Confidential

WAR DIARY OF 210th Field Company R.E.
MAJOR EDWARD HOPPER R.E.

FROM August 1st TO August 31st 1916.

WAR DIARY or INTELLIGENCE SUMMARY

Army Form C. 2118

Place	Date	Hour	Summary of Events and Information	Remarks and references to Appendices
R.36a 6.8	Aug 1st to Aug 31st 1916.		Repairs to FRONT LINE. General R.E. work including Construction of 292 U frames. Inspection of sites & and advice on materials required for gun emplacements and ammunition dumps. Repairs to pumps and water tanks in FRONT AREA. Refreshment to be at Crown Barrier. Construction of war prisoners Enclosure. Collection and blowing up of Enemy shells. Improvements to Trolleys. Improvements to Horse Standings. On the 26th - Aug. Divisional instruction 31 Div 5609 was received and from the 27th inst 2 Sections of this Company have been engaged on the primary works - after consolidation with B.G. 94th Brigade. 2 trench Battalion H.Q. 7 medical dug out (already mentioned) 2 bomb stores - 2 ration dumps - 2 water dumps 2 S.A.A. dumps.	

Ebstephanie
COMMANDING
210TH FIELD COMPANY R.E.

Army Form C. 2118.

WAR DIARY
or
INTELLIGENCE SUMMARY
(Erase heading not required.)

Place	Date	Hour	Summary of Events and Information	Remarks and references to Appendices
R 36 a 6. 8	Aug 1st to Aug 31st 1916		During this month the 210th Field Company has been employed on the following works. Reconstructing "B" line between PIONEER and LANSDOWNE. Constructing new trench known to HUSH HALL SWITCH connecting "B" line with B1 Divisional support. Construction and section of foundation for O.P. (Imitation tree) in PLUM STREET. Cleaning out, draining, repairing, replacing trench boards and revetting in COVERED WAY, BALUCHI, NEW CUT, GUARDS and LANSDOWNE. Erection of 4 DUGOUTS (X1 corps types) in "B" line - one (only) Baby Elephant dugout carried with concrete in front line. Since baby elephant dugouts in FRONT LINE - repair of 30 dugouts in FRONT LINE. Pad construction of 2 Battalion H.Q. dugouts and 1 medium dugout	

Wooper? RE
COMMANDING
210TH FIELD COMPANY R.E.

Army Form C. 2118

WAR DIARY
or
INTELLIGENCE SUMMARY
(Erase heading not required.)

Instructions regarding War Diaries and Intelligence Summaries are contained in F. S. Regs., Part II. and the Staff Manual respectively. Title Pages will be prepared in manuscript.

Place	Date	Hour	Summary of Events and Information	Remarks and references to Appendices

1875 Wt. W593/826 1,000,000 4/15 J.B.C. & A. A.D.S.S./Forms/C. 2118.

Confidential

War Diary

210 Field Coy R.E.

31st Division

September 1916.

Army Form C. 2118

WAR DIARY

~~INTELLIGENCE SUMMARY~~

(Erase heading not required.)

Instructions regarding War Diaries and Intelligence Summaries are contained in F.S. Regs., Part II. and the Staff Manual respectively. Title Pages will be prepared in manuscript.

Place	Date	Hour	Summary of Events and Information	Remarks and references to Appendices
R36.a. 6.8.	Sep 1st to Sep 16th		NEUVE CHAPELLE AREA. During this period (Sep. 1–16) the 210th Field Company has been employed on the following works. Construction of New trench from "B" line to B1 of -Bn. Support Clearing, cleaning, repairing, replacing trench boards & revetting the following Communication trenches. COVERED WAY, LANSDOWNE, COPSE, HAZARD, BALUCHI, CHATEAU ROAD. Reconstructing "B" line PIONEER & CRESCENT Paul construction of - Battalion H.Q. dug out with small dug outs for BOMBS, RATIONS, WATER & S.A.A., BUTE ST. Paul construction of B attachmn S.A. and medical aid dug outs - with small dug outs for signals, bombs, rations, water, S.A.A. & guard - LANSDOWNE & GUARDS TRENCH.	

WAR DIARY

Army Form C. 2118

(Erase heading not required.)

Instructions regarding War Diaries and Intelligence Summaries are contained in F.S. Regs., Part II. and the Staff Manual respectively. Title Pages will be prepared in manuscript.

Place	Date	Hour	Summary of Events and Information	Remarks and references to Appendices
R36a.68	Sep 1st to Sep 16th		Supervision of construction of Baby Elephant dugouts in Front line. Repairs to pumps HUSH HALL & PORT ARTHUR & trench pumps. Renewal of induction pipe O.P. off PLUM STREET. Formation of 3 R.E. dumps - at end of tram line behind RUE DE BOIS - off COPSE and off LANSDOWNE. Practice of 2 Sections in rapid wiring.	
GORRE	Sep 17th		Moved to GIVENCHY Sector - Company billeted at GORRE.	
	Sep 18th to Sep 30th		Repairs to following communication trench - WOLFE, ORCHARD, HERTS, CHEYNE WALK. Repairs to Battalion H.Q. and Brigade H.Q. HERTS AVENUE pumping station - putting in extra tank - making foot approaches to pumping station & general repairs.	

Army Form C. 2118

WAR DIARY

or

~~INTELLIGENCE SUMMARY~~

(Erase heading not required.)

Instructions regarding War Diaries and Intelligence Summaries are contained in F. S. Regs., Part II. and the Staff Manual respectively. Title Pages will be prepared in manuscript.

Place	Date	Hour	Summary of Events and Information	Remarks and references to Appendices
GORRE	Sep 18th to Sep 30th		Construction of dicholding O.P. PONTFIXE - Completed. Pad Construction of O.P. GUNNERS SIDING north of WOLFE ROAD. Pad construction of O.P. QUEENS ROAD - loop holes in KINGS ROAD. Construction of I.T. with two dugouts Completed. Construction of TRENCH MORTAR Emplacement frame for 231 Battery concrete. Construction of 120 slabs for covering dugouts. Construction of notice boards & sign posts. Repairs to under water bridge 200yds behind front line at CHEYNE WALK. SANDBAGGING of and general repairs to LONG FARM dressing station.	

WAR DIARY
or
~~INTELLIGENCE SUMMARY~~
(Erase heading not required.)

Army Form C. 2118

Place	Date	Hour	Summary of Events and Information	Remarks and references to Appendices
GORRE	Sep 18 to Sep 30		Repairs three troughs Artillery horse lines BETHUNE. Superiors prepared in front line.  ElSophmayvile O.C. 210th F.C.R.E.	

CONFIDENTIAL

War Diary
of
Edward Hopper - Major R.E. 210TH FLD.Co RE

From October 1st 1916 to October 31st 1916

Volume 8

Vol 8

Volume 10

Army Form C. 2118

WAR DIARY
or
INTELLIGENCE SUMMARY
(Erase heading not required.)

Instructions regarding War Diaries and Intelligence Summaries are contained in F. S. Regs., Part II. and the Staff Manual respectively. Title Pages will be prepared in manuscript.

Place	Date	Hour	Summary of Events and Information	Remarks and references to Appendices
GIVENCHY	Oct 1 to Oct 4		Four sections working in forward area.	
"	Oct 5		Company marched from GORRE to BUSNES.	
BUSNES	Oct 8		Company marched from BUSNES to LILLERS and entrained for DOULLENS.	
DOULLENS	Oct 9		Detrained at DOULLENS and marched to THIEVRES.	
THIEVRES	Oct 12		2 Sections Nos 2 & 4 moved to SAILLY for work in forward area	
"	Oct 13		HQs and 2 sections Nos 1 & 3 marched from THIEVRES to COIGNEUX.	
COIGNEUX	Oct 14		No 4 Section returned from SAILLY to COIGNEUX.	
"	Oct 16		HQs & No 1 Section moved to HEBUTURNE	
HEBUTURNE	Oct 17		HQs & No 1 Section returned to COIGNEUX being relieved	
COIGNEUX	Oct 17 to Oct 24		No 2 section moving from Sailly. No 2 section working in forward area. Nos 1 & 3 r 4 section in back area.	

Army Form C. 2118

WAR DIARY
or
INTELLIGENCE SUMMARY
(Erase heading not required.)

Instructions regarding War Diaries and Intelligence Summaries are contained in F.S. Regs., Part II. and the Staff Manual respectively. Title Pages will be prepared in manuscript.

Place	Date	Hour	Summary of Events and Information	Remarks and references to Appendices
COIGNEUX	Oct. 21st		No 3 Section moved from COIGNEUX to HEBUTERNE	
	Oct. 21st to Oct. 31st		The two Sections at HEBUTERNE working under orders of Brigadier GENERAL – being engaged on dug outs – in FUSILIER & VERGINGETORIX & repairs to communication trenches. The two sections at COIGNEUX working under orders of XIII Corps. have been engaged on water supply by 4" pipe line DELL to HEBUTERNE (3000 YDS Completed). Erection of 2 – 8000 galls tanks (canvas) at COIGNEUX water point – Erection of stand pipes – Repaired road gutters and road sections of Engine house – foundation for heavy weather Engine. Erection of boiler – Chimney etc. + 9 several works including section of platform for heavy howitzer. Repair of decauville tramway – repairs & Coy Ammunition dugdump.	

E. Boston Major RE

31/ 210 F.C Eng
YD79

War Diary of
Edward Hopper Major R.E.

Volume XI

from 1st November 1916 to
30 November 1916

Confidential

Place	Date	Hour	Summary of Events and Information	Remarks and references to Appendices
COIGNEUX	Nov 1st to Nov 4th		2 Sections (3 & 4) living in HEBUTERNE work in forward area	
	Nov 4th 1916		These two sections invalidated to SAILLY. They have been employed on the erection of two NISSEN huts, had for Officers, cook house latrines etc in their camp at SAILLY - clearing bench boardings to REVEL, JEAN BART, NAIRNE - making stumps in REVEL and clearing & repairing JENA - Construction of floors deck dug outs in Du GOESCLIN & JENA - Erection of huts & construction of horse standings for 94th Brigade HQ at SAILLY.	
			The two sections (1 & 2) living in COIGNEUX have been employed in laying 4" pipe (DELL & HEBUTERNE) 1500 yds completed. Completion of pump & boiler house at COIGNEUX - connecting up boiler with pump - making connections from canvas bath to water pond at COIGNEUX - Repairing and cleaning huts at K.14.a. Central - laying Decauville feed	

WAR DIARY
INTELLIGENCE SUMMARY
(Erase heading not required.)

Army Form C. 2118

Place	Date	Hour	Summary of Events and Information	Remarks and references to Appendices
			for 153 Siege battery at SAILLY 1490 yds completed. Repairs to and covering in Stables A162 battery R.F.A. SLEGER. Repairs to billet Indian Cavalry COIGNEUX — Repairs to hut including bolting in windows for 32nd H.A.G. Section of Canvas tanks at J.1.d 9.2 & J.8.c 8.8. Tarring & these tanks. Stack at ORGNEUX. Section of horse troughs. Laying Facine road at COIN. Repairs to hutments at BAYENCOURT. Construction of DECAUVILLE track for 154 Siege battery 350 yds. completed with loading stage. Laying of YELLOW LINE from hut of KELLERMAN K.3.c.4.3 to WELCOME K.16.b.0.5.9.0 — Inner line 2200 yds completed Second line 1650 yds. completed (550 yds of this line was completed when the C.C. commenced work) Radiating lines for machine guns 850 yds completed — width of lines 7army — 5 yds.	

Wolfe Shape RE
COMMANDING
210TH FIELD COMPANY R.E.

War Diary of A.B. Clough Major R.E.
from 1st December 1916 to 31st December 1916

2/10 Fd Coy
1/10 Fd Coy

Volume 18.

WAR DIARY
or
INTELLIGENCE SUMMARY

(Erase heading not required.)

Army Form C. 2118

Vol 12

Place	Date	Hour	Summary of Events and Information	Remarks and references to Appendices
COIGNEUX.	1/2		Wiring of Yellow Line completed by deep dug outs & clearing & deepening trenches	
		3ᵈ–9ᵗʰ	Nᵒˢ 1 & 2 Recce. Repairing Billets for the Company, rebuilding dugouts at BAYENCOURT & constructing huts for 93ʳᵈ Bde Sta. Nᵒˢ 3 & 4 Recce. White Red Bde infront of BRISOUX & OBER. Wiring & clearing & repairing trenches continued, also	
		9ᵗʰ–31ˢᵗ	Continued work in front line including JENA, GUESCLIN deep dug outs, tres large elephant shelters in GETRIX and the clearing & duckboarding of JENA C.T. from BRISOUX – KNOX. Nᵒˢ 2 & 3 Rec. Country & repairing Billets in BAYENCOURT, also shelving Bolt utimate range Rifle Range. Nᵒ COIGNEUX, & Church Army Hut was erected, also a draft Ryans and huts in COIGNEUX camp were repaired.	
			NOTE. Nᵒ 2. Section Nᵒ 4 in front line under Lt #27 ½ R.E.F.F. 600 tiles have been carried into the Emplacement entire period for indicator Stacks, X.P.M Bundles for revetting, trench frame stores, mining cases. The Major O.B.Clive R.E finished the Company on the 24ᵗʰ to 25ᵗʰ, where command of the Company was Major E. HOPPER, R.E. General Purlin has been employed a great deal in Transport of stores	

O.B.Clive R.E
Major R.E.
27/4/15
O.C. 210 Coy R.E.

Confidential

Volume XIII.

Vol XI

War Diary.

210th Field Company. R.E. 31st Division

January 1917.

Army Form C. 2118.

Vol. II.

WAR DIARY
or
INTELLIGENCE SUMMARY.
(Erase heading not required.)

Instructions regarding War Diaries and Intelligence Summaries are contained in F. S. Regs., Part II. and the Staff Manual respectively. Title pages will be prepared in manuscript.

Place	Date	Hour	Summary of Events and Information	Remarks and references to Appendices
COIGNEUX	1–4		Nos. 1 & 2 Coys on ground work in the line under 94 I.B. Coys 3 & 4 up to Sausage Gully & France, doing despatching of dugouts, wire etc.	
	5th		Nos. 3 & 4 on back work. Bn. Hq. Billets in BAYENCOURT. Workshops lorries & Nissen huts.	
	6–7th & 8		Nos. 1 & 3 Coys proceeded to GEZAINCOURT to start Nissen huts under 186 Inf Bde. Nos. 2 & 4 continued work in the line in BAYENCOURT & COIGNEUX	
	9th		Nos. 2 & 4 as above. Handed over work to strengthened 94 Inf Bde. Railway bailey pit depart to meet	
OCCOCHES	10–15		H.Q. Bn, Coys 2, 3, & 4 proceeded to OCCOCHES by light railway transport gear. Accommodated in NISSEN huts. Nos. 2 & 4 doing NISSEN huts, Billets, entrances to approaches in GEZAINCOURT	
GEZAINCOURT	16th		Nos. 1 & 2 Coys proceeded to GEZAINCOURT to carry on putting up Nissen huts. Coys 3 Bn left at OCCOCHES to continue locating of horse standing & huts and billets as above.	
-	17–21		No. 4 from No. 1 R. at GEZAINCOURT.	
	22			
	23rd 24th		Nos. 2 & 3 Bns commenced training programmes, musketry & equipment & modell fighting at GEZAINCOURT	

WAR DIARY
or
INTELLIGENCE SUMMARY.

Army Form C. 2118.

Place	Date	Hour	Summary of Events and Information	Remarks and references to Appendices
	25th		No 4 Sec returned to OUCOCHES to continue existing River Standings and huts. Nos 1,2 & 3 continued training.	
	26/27		Work as above, including River Standings at GEZAINCOURT.	
	28th		Sec Engr. forwarded tracing to mort'ying to BEAUSSART to replace 5b" & 4 big R.E. huts in Yellow Line under C.E. V Corps.	
	29, 30 31st		Work on Yellow Line in front of BEAUMONT HAMEL. Instruction preparing M G emplacements & deep dug outs for permanent MG emplacements.	

R.B. [signature] Capt RE
OC 210 [Field Coy] RE

210 FIELD COMPANY
FEB 2 1917
ROYAL ENGINEERS

Confidential

Volume XIV

Vol 14

War Diary.

210th Field Coy R.E. 31st Division

February 1917.

Army Form C. 2118

Vol.14

WAR DIARY
or
INTELLIGENCE SUMMARY
(Erase heading not required.)

Instructions regarding War Diaries and Intelligence Summaries are contained in F.S. Regs., Part II. and the Staff Manual respectively. Title Pages will be prepared in manuscript.

Place	Date	Hour	Summary of Events and Information	Remarks and references to Appendices
BEAUSSART	1/2/17 to 3/17		All Sections working on Yellow Line in front of BEAUMONT HAMEL, constructing emplacements and dug outs. Water direct under V Corps. H.Q. at BEAUSSART.	M.G.
—	4/17		Orders to move. Packing up, cleaning vehicles, gear etc.	
BERNAVILLE	5/17		The Company moved by Motor Lorry to BERNAVILLE. Transport went right through in one day.	
—	6/17		Erecting Nissen Huts for own use, also Purchasing By Billets.	
—	7/17		No.1 Sec. moved to CANDAS for work. Constructing of Nissen Huts + Bath Rooms at CANDAS + FIENVILLERS. No.2 Sec. Purchasing Nissen Huts etc at BERNAVILLE. No.3 Sec. erecting Nissen Shelters at the Ry. No.4 Sec split up for work at VIEUZECOURT, BOISBERGUES, AUTHIEUX + LE MEILLARD, on erection of Baths, Nissen Huts etc.	
—	8/17		Work as above. All tool carts thoroughly overhauled, explosives etc tested throughout.	
—	9/17		Work as above. Instruction afternoon.	
—	10/17		—	
—	11/17		—	
—	12/17		—	
—	16/17		—	
—	17/17		— Half day off.	
—	18/17		Nos 1 + 4 Secs returned to H.Q. + packed up.	
BEAUVAL	19/17		Marched to BEAUVAL + billeted for the night.	

Army Form C. 2118

WAR DIARY
or
INTELLIGENCE SUMMARY
(Erase heading not required.)

Instructions regarding War Diaries and Intelligence Summaries are contained in F.S. Regs., Part II. and the Staff Manual respectively. Title Pages will be prepared in manuscript.

Place	Date	Hour	Summary of Events and Information	Remarks and references to Appendices
COIGNEUX	20/2/17		Marched via BEAUQUESNE, MARIEUX, RAUTHIE to COIGNEUX, + moved in to Hutted camp near R.E. Park.	
—	21/2/17		Work in R.E. Park - Carp., repairing huts and bunks.	
—	22/2/17		Drainage of Camp + erecting huts, latrines etc.	
—	23/2/17		Work on erection of NISSEN huts at COIGNEUX + COUIN. Return at COUIN Pumping Station at HEBUTERNE + COIGNEUX (two). Electric Pumping Station + R.E.Park. Work as above. Also construction of dug outs in GUESSIN TR.	
—	24/2/17		No 2 Sec. moved to THIÈVRES.	
—	25/2/17		HQ remained at COIGNEUX. On 1.3.17 been moved to HEBUTERNE for work on SERHEB rd. Md. One to relieved of enemy. Continue work commenced at 4.30 p. No 3 Sec. hung to the Caves. No 2 Sec. returned at COIGNEUX.	
—	26/2/17		No 1.3.17 on construction work on SERHEB rd. No 2 Sec. on R.E. Park material Arty. Bridge.	
—	27/2/17		No 1.3.17 Sect. worked blower shifts in SERHEB rd. which is in sight of enemy observation after as FUSILIER TR. No 2 Sec. went to HEBUTERNE to relieve No 3 which returned to COIGNEUX.	

27/2/17

Confidential

Volume XV

WD/13

War Diary.

210th Field Company R.E. 31st Division

March 1917.

Army Form C. 2118

WAR DIARY
or
INTELLIGENCE SUMMARY
(Erase heading not required.)

Vol 15

Instructions regarding War Diaries and Intelligence Summaries are contained in F.S. Regs., Part II. and the Staff Manual respectively. Title Pages will be prepared in manuscript.

Place	Date	Hour	Summary of Events and Information	Remarks and references to Appendices
COIGNEUX	1/3/17 to 3/3/17		Secs. 1, 2 & 4 living in HEBUTERNE Caves & working on improvement of SERHEB road. Sec 3 working in R.E. Park making Artillery OB rdys, etc.	
COLINCAMPS	4/3/17		Secs 1 & 2 moved from HEBUTERNE Caves to dug into in HITTITE TR. 1/2 & No 3 moved to COLINCAMPS to prepare Billets. No 2 & No 3 to HITTITE dugout. No 4 in R.E. Park.	
—	5/3/17		Report of road from LA SIGNY FM to OBSERVATION WOOD to JOHN COPSE. Construction Trench Board road. Revetting dugouts from OBSERVATION WOOD - STAR WOOD.	
—	6/3/17		Reconnaissance for constructing Decauville Track from JEAN BART line. Repair of & clearing trench boards North of above line. Erecting photograph for Alley watering facility. For well in dugout at STAR WOOD. No 4 to CURERIE.	
—	7/3/17 to 8/3/17		Commenced work on above. Observation as above.	
COLINCAMPS	9/3/17		HQ moved to COLINCAMPS.	
—	10/3/17		Work on COURCELLES dump, reports re gun etc. Tramway advanced 92 dump at STAR WOOD; carried on construction of new tramline & Decce Board Starts as above.	
—	11/3/17		As above — Also reconnaissance of German dug outs.	
—	14/3/17		Erected 3 NISSEN huts at EUSTIN, STAR WOOD as above.	
—	17/3/17		Completed tram line to group of old German dugouts just N.E. of STAR WOOD. Also con- pleted trench board road from OBSERVATION WOOD to JOHN COPSE. Group at STAR WOOD	

Army Form C. 2118.

Vol 15 (contd)

WAR DIARY
or
INTELLIGENCE SUMMARY.

(Erase heading not required.)

Instructions regarding War Diaries and Intelligence Summaries are contained in F. S. Regs., Part II. and the Staff Manual respectively. Title pages will be prepared in manuscript.

Place	Date	Hour	Summary of Events and Information	Remarks and references to Appendices
OLINCAMPS	18/3/17		WOOD run in orderly order. All ranks returned to H.Q.	
BEAUVAL	19/3/17		Packing and cleaning wagons	
VACQUERIE	20/3/17		Attached to 94th Bde Grp. Marched to BEAUVAL	
GAUCHIN	21/3/17		Marched to VACQUERIE.	
CAUCHY	22/3/17		" " GAUCHIN.	
---	23/3/17		" " CAUCHY.	
BOURECQ	24/3/17		Rest.	
ST VENANT	25/3/17		Marched to BOURECQ.	
	26/3/17		" " ST. VENANT.	
	27/3/17		Cleaning wagons etc. Drill No 1 Sec Surrendered Letters in discipline Punished by 20.	
	28/3/17		Bridges with Welsh Regts. Demolitions. Drill. Letters throwing away ammunition Punts. 5 No 2 surrendered No kit	
	29/3/17		Drill. Pontoon - Map reading + work in nature.	
	30/3/17		As above, also manoeuvres. Putting + Garting etc.	
	31/3/17			

R.B. Clm Stuffs
2/Lt 2nd WelCy

A5834 Wt. W4973 M687 750,000 8/16 D. D. & L. Ltd. Forms/C.2118/13.

Confidential

Volume XVI
Apl 14

War Diary.

210th Field Coy R.E. 31st Division

April 1917.

210/4090

Vol. 16.

Army Form C. 2118.

WAR DIARY
or
INTELLIGENCE SUMMARY.

Place	Date	Hour	Summary of Events and Information	Remarks and references to Appendices
ST VENANT	1/7/17		Rest day. Inspection of Kit etc. & Church Parade.	
—	2/7/17 to 6/7/17		Training. Pontooning, bailing out Strong Point, overhauling of night Repair huts.	
—	7/7/17		Packing up & clearing up of horse Killing in all breeds.	
GONNEHEM	8/7/17		Bn'n marched to GONNEHEM.	
—	9/7/17		Drill, Physical exercise etc.	
—	10/7/17			
BRUAY	11/7/17		Route march to BRUAY	
BARLIN	12/7/17		— BARLIN	
VILLERS BRULIN	13/7/17		— VILLERS BRULIN	
"	14/7/17		Payres & Rifle drill. Inspection under. Inspection of Girder Bridge section	
"	15/7/17		at SAVY dump by G.O.C.	
ECOIVRES	16/7/17		Route march to ECOIVRES	
ROCLINCOURT	17/7/17 18/7/17		— G.4.a.1.8 near ROCLINCOURT. 4 Store tents + 2 Bell tents provided. Attached for work direct under C.E. XIII Corps.	

Vol. 16.

Army Form C. 2118.

WAR DIARY
or
INTELLIGENCE SUMMARY.
(Erase heading not required.)

Instructions regarding War Diaries and Intelligence Summaries are contained in F.S. Regs., Part II. and the Staff Manual respectively. Title pages will be prepared in manuscript.

Place	Date	Hour	Summary of Events and Information	Remarks and references to Appendices
ROCLINCOURT	19/4/17		Laying out site for NISSEN hut camp for 18th, 5th men sent to 230 A.T. Coy	
"	20/4/17		for motor supply.	
"	21/4/17		Commenced erecting huts.	
"	22/4/17		Six huts allotted to 63 D.H.Q. Commenced erection of Latrines, Cookhouses etc.	
	23		Camp continued as above; 2 polies working on return of LENS area A.S. Wood. 4 men to 230 Coy for work on carpt department	
	24			
	25			
	26			
	27			
	28th 6.30		Our 1, 3, & 4 Secns. arr above. No. 2. Commenced erection of Divl H.Q. camp (NISSEN huts) at ROCLINCOURT (G.5b.2.7)	

2/5/17

Confidential

Volume XVII

J.15

War Diary.

210th Field Coy. R.E.

31st Division

May 1917.

WAR DIARY or INTELLIGENCE SUMMARY

Army Form C. 2118.

Vol. 17

Place	Date	Hour	Summary of Events and Information	Remarks and references to Appendices
ROCLINCOURT	1/5 to 3/5		Continued work on section of Div. H.Q. Ruttments at ROCLIN COURT. Provided guides for forming forward R.E. dumps East of BAILLEUL. Bosh in camp constructing 200 Statches.	
	4/5		Work on Div H.Q. as above. Work on Div H.Q. as above. 1 Sec erecting horse watering troughs at ANZIN. Repairs to windlass of well in Glena Lines.	
	5/5			
	6/5		No 4 Sec provided deflind area, dug out in Railway cutting at B26C for front line work. Other work as above. No 2 - (+o.c.f.CS.M)	
	7/5			
	8/5		No 1 Sec. erecting shelters for expert Accommodation in Railway cutting. No 2+4 on night work, constructing new shelters near front line (OPPY WOOD). No 3 erecting new Batts horse line at ANZIN.	
	9/5		Casualty on 9/5 1.O.R. Shrapnel in hand	
	10/5		As above. 7 Casualties to O.R. (for prisoning) on way up to front line.	
	11/5		No 1 Sec forward to forward area, No 2+4 returned to camp. No 3 ment at ANZIN. Batts. front line work, improvement of front line in front of OPPY WOOD.	
	12/5		No 3 moved to forward area + worked in front line with No 1. No 2+4 in Batts ANZIN.	
	13/5		No 1 constructed string front on edge of road west of GAVRELLE windmill. Others work as above.	
	14/5		No 1+3 consolidated ties existing posts round the 2 side of Windmill. No 2 commenced electric to horse troughs at G15 c 3.5. in ARRAS. No 4 a Batts ANZIN.	
			Casualties to D.R. 3. near windmill. (wounded, bullet + shrapnel). No 2 relieved No 1 at forward area.	
	15/5			
	16/5		No 4 forward to forward area. No 1 others as work in Batts. New posts commenced just west of windmill. No 3 working on improvement of OUSE C.T.	
	17/5		Casualties on 16/5 2 O.R. Killed. 2 O.R. wounded. On 17/5 1 O.R. gas-prisoning	

WAR DIARY or INTELLIGENCE SUMMARY

Army Form C. 2118.

(Erase heading not required.)

Place	Date	Hour	Summary of Events and Information	Remarks and references to Appendices
ROCLINCOURT	18/5 19/5		Nos 2 & 4 on front line work, connecting up posts East of windmill at GAVRELLE. No 1 in Baths at ANZIN. No 3 on OUSE C.T. moving back to HQ in 19th evening.	
	20/5		Nos 2 & 4 returned to HQ. 31st Div relieved by 63rd Div. Trenches line handed over to 249 Field Coy. No 1 completing Baths at ANZIN.	
	21/5		Rest	
	22/5		Whole Company working on Green Line, with 93rd I.B.	
	23/5 24/5		Whole Company working on Green Line under Corps.	
	25/5		Rest. 94th I.B. relieves 93rd I.B. Coys with 93rd I.B.	
	26/5 27/5		Rest. 94th I.B. believes 93rd I.B. to work on Green Line.	
	28/5 29/5 30/5		Whole Company working on Green Line. Coys now with 94th I.B.	
	31/5		Rest. Monthly relief at Company HQ Gys(?) on transport lines. 51 B.N.M.	

O/B Clof Maytre(?)
4th Coy RE
RE 210

Confidential

Volume XVIII

V57/6

War Diary.

210th Field Company R.E.

June 1917.

WAR DIARY
or
INTELLIGENCE SUMMARY.

(Erase heading not required.)

Army Form C. 2118.

VOL. 18.

Instructions regarding War Diaries and Intelligence Summaries are contained in F. S. Regs., Part II. and the Staff Manual respectively. Title pages will be prepared in manuscript.

Place	Date	Hour	Summary of Events and Information	Remarks and references to Appendices
ROCLINCOURT	1/6/17 to 4/6/17		Nos 1, 2, 3 Secs on Green Line defences. Not working in improvement of OUSE C.T.	
	5/6/17		Rest day	
	6/6/17 7/6/17 8/6/17		Work on Green Line, and C.T's forward to Red Line	
	9/6/17		Rest day	
	10/6/17		Preparation for takes over work in line from 63rd Div	
	11/6/17 12/6/17		Constructing hut & dug out for G.O.C. Improvement of Mule track near Bn HQ. Electric light fitted for Stores & erection of Rifle Range & Bivl. Area	
	13/6/17 14/6/17		No 1 Sec. digging new C.T., OUSE TR from VISCOUNT TR to ? tunnel. B" Hd Sec 2, 3+4 to Alone.	
	15/6/17			
	16/6/17		Commenced forming ? dump near BAILLEUL EAST Post for ? platoon. OUSE CT continued by No 3 sec. No 4 + ? Cinema, ? ?	
	17/6/17		No 1 constructing tank shelters to forward Sector. No 2 ? Cinema & ? ? No 3 in OUSE CT & No 4 construct 3 Baby Elephant shelters for Adv B" HQ in MARINE TR.	
	18/6/17		Ditto.	
	19/6/17 20/6/17		No 4 continued work on shelters in front line. No 3 constructs ? in ? ? in forward sector. No 2 ? Adv B" dump.	
	21/6/17		No 1 work Cinema. No 2 making ? posts in MARINE T.R. No 4 ? in shelters in MARINE	
	22/6/17		forward Sector continued. +3.	
	23/6/17		No 2 employed in Ad? Pits. No 3+4 work in B" HQ shelters by reliefs. No 1 making tramway.	

Army Form C. 2118.

WAR DIARY
or
INTELLIGENCE SUMMARY.
(Erase heading not required.)

Instructions regarding War Diaries and Intelligence Summaries are contained in F. S. Regs., Part II. and the Staff Manual respectively. Title pages will be prepared in manuscript.

Place	Date	Hour	Summary of Events and Information	Remarks and references to Appendices
ROCLINCOURT	24/6/17		Nos 1 in trenches. Nos 2 + 3 Rest. No 4 continued on B. HQ. posten (confined)	
	25/6/17		1 + 2 + 3 --- No 4 Rest.	
	26/6/17		No 2 in trenches. No 4 however went to Cinema + Bull cage. No 1 + 3 listening in trenches of trenches	
	27/6/17		Nos 1 + 3 + OC moved to Railway cutting dug out for wire in connection with operations employed in night 27/28. Clearing out forward trenches down to by ordee fire. No 2 in down + 2 in forward billets. No 4 in Bull cage + canteen.	
	28/6/17		No 1 + 3 standing by. Employed in night 25/29 clearing operations during cable line.	
	29/6/17		No 1 + 3 returned to Camp in afternoon (Roulincourt) No 2 in forward forward billets. No 4 in Café + canteen	
	30/6/17		No 1 + 3 Rest. Inspection J.C. Batts/etc. No 2 up in forward billets. No 4 in canteen cafe	

1/7/17

G.B. C. Ingoldby
Lt Col
OC 2nd Coy RE

ORIGINAL.

CONFIDENTIAL.

War Diary
of
210th Field Company. R. E.

from July 1st.1917 to July 31st.1917.

VOLUME ~~XXIII~~ XIX

* * * * * * * * * *

WAR DIARY or INTELLIGENCE SUMMARY

Army Form C. 2118.

Vol 17

Place	Date	Hour	Summary of Events and Information	Remarks and references to Appendices
ROCLINCOURT	1/7/17		2 Sections formed. Refitting etc into etc. 2 sections had working in Divisional Dump + Sailles & instructing Hulhamens	
	2/7/17		skg start of Musketry Rifle range etc.	
-"-	3/7/17		Preparing for mine heading. Working Parties for L. See moved to ECOIVRES to lately over Rifles + work under C.R.E. Corps Troops.	
ECOIVRES	4/7/17		HQ + No 1+3 moved to ECOIVRES. No 2 went to ANZIN for construction of Coal Siding.	
	5/7/17		Commenced work letting new from 247 Yd Ry. Repairs to from at ANZIN, erection of Camp at ECOIVRES for Chinese Labour Corps	
-"-	6/7/17		No 1. proceeded to FLORINGHEM for work. Elect at AUCHY sector. extension of Chinese Corps Beloved.	
	7/7-11/7		work proceeded as above. RBD outbury asked for 2 wired + about ECOIVRES. Chinese Camp completed on 15th	
	12/7		Drill all morning	
	13/7		HQ + whole Coy moved to HQtaimt with from 3rd Canadian Field Coy in ANNEVILLE sector. Camp at A14 a. 3.9.	
AU RIETZ (Alb. a. 3.9.)	13/7		No 1+3 Secs went forward dug outs for work in the line. from 2,4 Secs paid Reconnaissance of line.	
	14/7		Reconnaissance of line. Retubing structures in camp.	
	15/7		Commenced construction of AID POST for Duglas Battn. way to Elephant erection. Building of Battn Elephants. No 4 Sec. intent to forward dug out in VANCOUVER Lined in a good dug out. No 2 + 4 constructing [Engineers of commander said not over Chinese there + surround structures]	
	16/7		No 1 Paid at 2 hrs ETI. from QUEBEC to new front line	
-"-	19/7		No 1 Related by No 2 + work continued.	
	20/7/17		Reconnaissance of AID POST. Working of HUDSON + GRUS	
	21/7		+ constructing AID POST. Working of HUDSON + GRUS	
	22/7		No 4 relieved No 3 + carried on.	
	23/7/17		ground work on AID POST, Digging trench found up HUDSON, cleansing constructing of further dugs Per Ground + CTJ. On 3 Sets	
	5/29/17		Park water levels in Dis Baths near NEWVILLE ST VAAST, Humes Sandhp. Repairs stations for forward work etc.	
	30/17		No 1 Relieved by 2. Commenced Dires Store at AU RIETZ.	
	31/7/17		to 3 " " 4.	

ORIGINAL.

CONFIDENTIAL.

WAR DIARY

of

210th Field Company.R.E.

From 1/8/17 to 31/8/17.

VOLUME XX

Vol. 20

Army Form C. 2118.

WAR DIARY
or
INTELLIGENCE SUMMARY.
(Erase heading not required.)

Instructions regarding War Diaries and Intelligence Summaries are contained in F. S. Regs., Part II. and the Staff Manual respectively. Title pages will be prepared in manuscript.

Place	Date	Hour	Summary of Events and Information	Remarks and references to Appendices
AUX RIETZ	1/5/17		Nos 1-3 Secs. on forward work. Party mend ponds in TICKLER + HUDSON C.T. Nos 2+4 work + officer Standby and finer Stores. Also work in AID POST	
	2/5/17 3/5/17 4/5/17 5/5/17 6/5/17		No 2. Repair of entrances to THELUS caves. Remainder as above	
	7/5/17 8/5/17 9/5/17		Aid Post amplified. No 2 relieved No 1. No 3. No 2 worked int. Roof Bridges for revetted sides for sump [?] of dugouts. No 4 fixing gas shelters in Pole Ross.	
	10/5/17		Work as above.	
	11/5/17		No 1 constructing Gul Bins near LA TARGETTE + repairing habes points. No 2 commenced revetting TRIUMPH. No 4 commenced new Aid Post (René Stephant)	
	12/5/17 14/5/17		Asabove. Also No 2 fixing comfs in HUDSON + revetting B.2. shelters in front line.	
	15/5/17		No 1 relieved No 2. No 4 erecting Bridge over HUDSON	
	16/5/17 17/5/17-20 21/5/17		No 3 = No 4 - but continued as above. River Standpipes at by site under construction. No blower permits.	
	21/5/17		No 4 prepared charges for demolition of Steel Bridge at Embankment near FARBUS.	
	22/5/17 23/5/17		Demolition of Bridge Clearing debris + girders from battery bridge. Detachment working in reverting TRIUMPH, fixing comforts in HUDSON, constructing Aid Post, Shelter Bel alléss in the front line. No 2 relieved No 1.	
	24/5/17 25/5/17		No 4 relieved No 3.	

Army Form C. 2118.

WAR DIARY
or
INTELLIGENCE SUMMARY.
(Erase heading not required.)

Place	Date	Hour	Summary of Events and Information	Remarks and references to Appendices
AUX RIETZ	26/5		(m) Horse Standing & making Dismountings Camp.	
			(n) 2. Revetting Posting in TRIUMPH, fixing camp in MUDSVN.	
			(n) 3. Construct Dugout & Hutments for M.O.	
	27/5		3. Constructing Horse Standings	
	30		(n) 1. Dismantled work in #000fs for 31 ARP.	
	31		(n) 1. About (n) 2. (n) 3. Dismantled work on horse Standings at ECURIE.	
			During this month 1 Coy of Worcesters Pioneers (RND) have attached for work in new CT near the Ridge, working under this Cny supervision	

2-9-17

Confidential

Volume XXI

Vol 19

War Diary.

210th Field Company. R.E.   31st Division

September. 1917.

WAR DIARY or INTELLIGENCE SUMMARY

Army Form C. 2118.

Vol. 21

Place	Date	Hour	Summary of Events and Information	Remarks and references to Appendices
AUX REITZ	1/17		No 1 Sec relieved No 2 in forward work. Excavation of TRIUMPH T.T. & construction of AID POST.	
	2/17		Construction of new horse standings at ECURIE.	
	3/17		No 3 Sec relieved No 4 in forward work. Constructing new tents for G.O.C.	
	4/17		In/on TRIUMPH continued. Putting in R.E. stores. Fixing anti-gas Blankets.	
	5/17		Commenced work on new Coy Camp ECURIE.	
	6/17		Horse Stands TRIUMPH ready. Electric lighting in dug-out. Tidying up TINY. Fixing gas blankets AID POST. Erecting horse standings & G.O.C.'s hut.	
ONWARDS ECURIE	10/17		No 2 Sec relieved No 1 in forward area. Spence's Bridge fired at from CANADA T.T. & LEWIS Work.	
	11/17		No 4 Sec moved up to intermediate camp & worked all night electric shelters for gunner clothing store	
	12/17		No 4 relieved No 3 Sec in forward area.	
	13/17		Commenced excavation of large Elephant shelters for B.L. Hd in WINNIPEG road. Shelter hut is above.	
	14/17		Dismantling new dug outs for R.P.W. branch & erecting to new site.	
	15/17		Work on TINY completed. Bridges erected at junction of CANADA & horse Road, Coy Camp or ECURIE continued	
	16/17		Work on new Sec H.Q. tents. Water tanks in place.	
	17/17		Commenced structure in dummy position.	
	18/17		Commenced Bomb Store for Bde in VANCOUVER road.	
	19/17		Repair of NISSEN huts ECURIE. Bomb store in VAN COUVER road completed. Ray huts etc Sump in TOTNES.	
	20/17		No 1 relieved No 2 in forward. Erecting Gage shelters + excavation in WINNIPEG road for B.L. shell. Work continued in TRIUMPH N & S, Coys funds in place etc.	

Army Form C. 2118.

WAR DIARY
or
INTELLIGENCE SUMMARY.
(Erase heading not required.)

Instructions regarding War Diaries and Intelligence Summaries are contained in F. S. Regs., Part II. and the Staff Manual respectively. Title pages will be prepared in manuscript.

Place	Date	Hour	Summary of Events and Information	Remarks and references to Appendices
	21/9		Construction of Ordnance Road at Refilling Point have continued in TOTNES, TRIUMPH & TICKLER firing trenches, dumps, B3 shelters etc. Horse standings, Coy Camp.	
	22/9		No 3 Relieved No 4 from aid	
	23/9		Commenced erecting Dummy Tank.	
	24/9 25/9		Gas Blankets fitted to M.G. dug outs. Ottawa and Regina. Preparing bridge over New MONTREAL TR.	
	26/9 27/9 &		Firing Points in New MONTREAL. Commenced erection of changing rooms at ECURIE Baths. Work continued as before in TOTNES, NOVA SCOTIA, TRIUMPH, new B" hut in WINNIPEG, Dummy Tank, ECURIE Baths.	
	30/9		Ordnance road at Refilling Point, erecting Horse lines for Bde Canteen	

3-10-17

A.B. Clark
Capt
OC 2.W. Can Engrs

Confidential

Volume XXII

WD 20

War Diary

210 Field Coy. R.E.   31st Division

October 1917

Army Form C. 2118.

WAR DIARY
or
INTELLIGENCE SUMMARY.
(Erase heading not required.)

VOL. 22

Instructions regarding War Diaries and Intelligence Summaries are contained in F.S. Regs., Part II. and the Staff Manual respectively. Title pages will be prepared in manuscript.

Place	Date	Hour	Summary of Events and Information	Remarks and references to Appendices
ECURIE	1/7/17 & 2/7/17		Nos 2 & 3 Secs on General work; completion of new B's HQ in WINNIPEG tunl. Facing Sumps in front line and construction of TRIUMPH tr. No 1 S4 on Road work at ECURIE Station, replacing front. Bde Transport line & clearing that up. Place hut at ACG. No 3 retuning to HQ.	
	3/7/17		Finished the west dummy figures. Move as above.	
	4/7/17 to 7/7/17		Commenced shelters for ARP, & also to form of ECURIE road camp. Preparing for Bn Rheams & accomodation. No 2 Sec. Ground-out tram Poles in front of Stables ready for drawing Stuff for Chamel & tables. No 3 B's HQ. Woodworking, revetting, emptying sump & to chalets in OUSE tr & Gr base in easting accomodation for BROWN Line	
	8/7/17 9/7/17		No 1 relieved No 2 General. Commenced repairing of tracks in Springfield Camp. Commenced erecting bunker accommodation in Red Line.	
	10/7/17			
	11/7/17 12 13/7/17		Commenced alteration & repair of the Blanchols in dug-out & dumps. Commenced hut on 94 Rd to HQ. Lining B's hut & making Shelter, also erecting NISSEN huts with further for Rheams.	
	14/7/17 15/7/17		Began installing HUDSON Tr after damage by hostile fire. Commenced hut in B'kfast Camp.	
	16/7/17 19/7/17		Commenced hut in B'kfast Camp. Charlie at ECURIE Lake. No 3 Wired No 1 on General work. Enlarging shelter B's HQ & reinforcing HUDSON. Trench hut at Bde H.Q. completed. One ensite on B&BS Camp. Accommodation for Rd line. Bringing Bath Chamber, ARP	
	20/7/17 21/7/17		No 2 Hhamed No 1 on Rd Line work & moved VANCOUVER road. Commenced erecting canopy protective walls to holes in WILLERVAL, also refastening new BBS in VANCOUVER road	

A5834 Wt. W4973/M687 750,000 8/16 D.D. & L.Ltd. Forms/C.2118/13.

Army Form C. 2118.

WAR DIARY
or
INTELLIGENCE SUMMARY.
(Erase heading not required.)

Instructions regarding War Diaries and Intelligence Summaries are contained in F. S. Regs., Part II. and the Staff Manual respectively. Title pages will be prepared in manuscript.

Place	Date	Hour	Summary of Events and Information	Remarks and references to Appendices
ECURIE	22/10 to 27/10		General Field work continued. On 10th. Stanwick Pat Guardroom, line & repairing HUDSON dugout & enlarged infantry enemy fire.	
	26/10		Sunday, rest day for Back sections. Commenced dismantling dugouts	
	29/10		Commenced work in NEW BRUNSWICK TR, preparing accommodation for 1 Coy Rifle Reserve & trench stores	
	30/10		Fired in Q.B.18 in Front Line. Work continued. No Infantry work.	
	31/10		No. 1 section No. 2 came to Red Line NEW BRUNSWICK and ADS.	

1-11-17

210th FIELD COMPANY ROYAL ENGINEERS NOV 1 1917

ORIGINAL.

CONFIDENTIAL.

War Diary

of

210th Field Company.R.E.

1/11/17   to   30/11/17

Volume XXIII.

WAR DIARY
or
INTELLIGENCE SUMMARY.

Army Form G. 2118.

VOL 23

Place	Date	Hour	Summary of Events and Information	Remarks and references to Appendices
ECURIE.	1/17 to 4/17		Nos 1 & 4 Secs general improvement of N.BRUNSWICK TR. Construction of ADS near WILLERVAL. Clearing & revetting HUDSON TR. Draining & erecting dug outs & shelters in CANADA TR. Nos 2 & 3 Recce on back work. Repairs to Springfield Camp. Constructing Disinfestation Chamber. Erecting huts for DADOS.	
	5/17.		No 2 Sec preparing bungalow. Trestles for rd. No 4 prepared routes & stepping in front line.	
	6/17.		Commenced erection of hand hut for canteen at Mr St ELOI.	
	9/17.		No 2 returned to forward work. Erection of Brittee shelters in WINNIPEG and	
	10/17 to 20/17.		rehieved No 1 in forward work. Erection of bridges over front line & near front line at various points for advance. History cut in MONTREAL TR. Erection of shelters for brigade in HUDSON at junction with Red Rue. Alterations as before.	
	21/17.		Handed over ACHEVILLE Section to Canadian Engineers. No 1 & 4 Secs moved to forward billets in OPPY sector. Nos 2 & 3 Secs returned to HQ.	
	22/17.		Officers & NCOs reconnoitring new line. Improvement of forward billets.	
	23/17.		Commenced new Sector. Improvements to OPPY & BRADFORD Posts. revetting & supports.	
	24/17.		Reclaimed Springfield Camp. DADOS Camp.	
	25/17.		Commenced canteen in JUSE TR. Excavation of new trench "BRUN."	
	26/17 to 29/17.		Work widening BEDFORD Rd in addition to other work. Parties of 10 attached to 211 Coy for similar work. Dummy figure (240 yds) erected in front of our front line near BRADFORD POST. Strength of Coy Officers 6, Bn Ranks 216 in addition to Infantry & Railway working parties.	
	30/17.		Commenced work in rear of ECURIE WOOD Camp.	3 12/17

A5834   Wt. W4973/M687 750,000 8/16 D.D. & L. Ltd. Forms/C.2118/13.

ORIGINAL.

CONFIDENTIAL.

WAR DIARY
of
210th Field Company.R.E.

From 1/12/17 to 31/12/17.

VOLUME XXIV.

WAR DIARY or INTELLIGENCE SUMMARY

Army Form C. 2118.

Vol. 24

Place	Date	Hour	Summary of Events and Information	Remarks and references to Appendices
ECURIE	1/12/17 to 5/12/17		Nos 1 & 4 Secs working with div. Revetting & improving OPPY & BRADFORD POSTS. Nos 2 & 3 Secs on Base work, repairs to Springvale Camp, construction of Runways & upkeep of MDS's camp etc.	
	6/12/17		Nos 1 & 4 Dismounted HQ began preparations to ready for moving.	
ST CATHERINE (ARRAS)	7/12/17		Moved to ST CATHERINE	
	8/12/17 to 12/12/17		Reorganising. Spent section of Coy H.Q. Inspection Parade at ANZIN. Lining, revetting, revetments. Lieuts J. Marshall and B.J. Bishop left the Company on transfer to Army/L. R. (am R. Corps)	
	13/12/17		Erection of Canteen and hut started at ROCLINCOURT. Erection of NISSEN huts at 4th NLA Vet Sec. No 4 Sec. proceeded to PERNES for work under C.E. XIII Corps.	
	14/12/17 to 20/12/17		Reorganization of Company. Lieuts J.C.B. Brackenford Jones & G.H. Bytes and II Lieut J.C.B. Brackenford Jones transferred to the Company at 15 days & Nelson.	
ECURIE	21/12		Returned to H.Q. Camp at ECURIE. No. 4 Sec returned from PERNES.	
	22/12/17		Continued work on Canteen. Commenced work on Command shelter in Lingheaut. Practical markings for mining.	
	23/12		Construction of Quartermaster's Wing.	
	24/12/17		Commenced work on Coy ORs Baths, new hut-up & Coy & Company HQ.	
	25/12		Xmas day. No work.	
	26/12 to 29/12		Destruction of unsafe ammunition at ARP. Clearance on slopes. Refurnish of OC's, huts & erection of NISSEN hut at S.H.B.	
	30/12/17		Commenced building protection shrine lines. Erection of NISSEN huts at ROUTH Camp.	
	31/12		Nos 2 & 4 Secs moved to forward Billets in Anzin.	

ORIGINAL.

CONFIDENTIAL.

WAR DIARY

of

210th Field Company.R.E.

1/1/18 to 31/1/18.

VOLUME XXV.

Army Form C. 2118.

Volume 25

WAR DIARY
or
INTELLIGENCE SUMMARY.

(Erase heading not required.)

Place	Date	Hour	Summary of Events and Information	Remarks and references to Appendices
ECURIE	1/8		2nd & 3rd Secs moved forward billets in LONGWOOD for work under XIII Corps	
	2/8		All 4 Secs improving billets in LONGWOOD. Continued first delay about of wiring. No 2 Lt. moved forward.	
	3/8		Preparing for Hq wiring along TOMMY ALLEY & TIRED ALLEY & conversion of trench into fire bay.	
	6/8			
	7/8		Commenced wiring according to Corps Scheme.	
	8/8		No 4 returned to H.Q. Party relieved by Sec of 223 H.Q.	
	10/8 13		Wiring & trench conversion continued	
	14/8		No 4 Sec relieved by 1 Sec.	
	15/8		No 1 Sec " " No 3 "	
	21/8			
	25/8		Wiring along TOMMY & TIRED completed. Battery wire in STATION & FARBUS Wood under construction.	
	26/8		Wiring in STATION & FARBUS WOOD + conversion of trench completed	
	27/8		No 2 Sec relieved to site.	
	28/8		No 1 & 4 Sec relieved to H.Q.	
	29/8		Rest day	
	30/8		No 2 Sec Corps tram line from R.E. Rume lines to Ramme dump to left & right. Ran the from D.A.C. Rue Shed to Ramme dump. W 1 Sec to Splinter proof shelter. Wound outer P.ork. No 3 Building protective noises wound shelter.	
	31/8			

A.B.Plenkingo 2
OC 210 FY Coy.

31/8

ORIGINAL.

CONFIDENTIAL.

War Diary

of

210th Field Company. R.E.

from 1/2/18 to 28/2/18.

VOLUME XXVI

WAR DIARY
or
INTELLIGENCE SUMMARY

Army Form C. 2118.

VOL # 26

Place	Date	Hour	Summary of Events and Information	Remarks and references to Appendices
ECURIE	1/2/18		Company at ECURIE and H.Q. for Section working or erection of bomb proof walls at Divisional H.Q. and tapping of Leauville Track at	
	4/2/18		the Horse Lines of several units in the Divison.	
	4/2/18		Sections 1 & 3 moves to LONGWOOD to recce work on XIII Corps Heavy Scheme. Sections 2 & 4 working on Roads serving LONGWOOD ROAD. Construction of Lt. Bde. H.Q. at BRENSSEY HILL. Construction of Bauls. Line Erections.	
	4/2/18		Work of Section continued as above.	
	10/2/18		Lt. H.F.A. KEATING to Field Corps Infantry School for 3 weeks course.	
	12/2/18		Sections 2 & 4 relieved Sections 1 & 3 at LONGWOOD and took charge	
	15/2/18		Sections 1 & 3 moves to LONGWOOD, the whole Company to work on XIIIth Corps Heavy Scheme.	
	15/2/18		Work on Kenny Entrances on the following Trenches - ANTELOPE ALLEY - STATION HOOD - FARBUS HOOD - G.P.R. & STATION HOOD to MERSEY TRENCH - HUDSON G.	
	22/2/18		Major A.B. CLOUGH R.E. Left the Company to take up appointment as Instructor at ALDERSHOT.	
	22/2/18		Work continues as above. Lt. JW. G. R.E. to be Acting O.C. to OC.	
	28/2/18		Work continues as above. Lt. JW. G. R.E. on 4/3/18 on appointment of new O.C. 210th Field Co. R.E.	

31st Divisional Engineers

WAR DIARY

210th FIELD COMPANY R. E.

MARCH 1918

ORIGINAL.

CONFIDENTIAL.

WAR DIARY.
of
210th Field Company. R.E.

From 1/3/18 to 31/3/18.

VOLUME XXVII

WAR DIARY or INTELLIGENCE SUMMARY

Army Form C. 2118.

VOL 27

Place	Date	Hour	Summary of Events and Information	Remarks and references to Appendices
ECURIE	1/3/18 to 3/3/18		Company continues work on the XIII Corps Swing Scheme at LONGWOOD and on the East Hand Gate returned to H.Q. ECURIE.	
	4/3/18		3½ Divn relieves but R.E. remains forward and moved to AUBREY CAMP to take over work in PURPLE ZONE. XIII Corps Swing Scheme.	
	4/3/18 to 10/3/18		Work continues in Purple Zone. Lt. EASTON JONES joins the Company.	
	11/3/18		Heavy shelled AUBREY CAMP. No casualties but Officers Mess and sleeping quarters damaged including Kits of Officers & Caps. Each night spent the night in Trenches alongside ARRAS - LENS ROAD.	
	11/3/18 to 21/3/18		Work continues in Purple Zone. Heavy shelled but no casualties. Company damage.	
	13/3/18		Lieut Ingham appointed Second in Command of the Company vice Lieut EASTON transferred to 223rd Field Company R.E. Acting rank of Captain	

Army Form C. 2118.

WAR DIARY
or
INTELLIGENCE SUMMARY.
(Erase heading not required.)

Instructions regarding War Diaries and Intelligence Summaries are contained in F. S. Regs., Part II. and the Staff Manual respectively. Title pages will be prepared in manuscript.

Place	Date	Hour	Summary of Events and Information	Remarks and references to Appendices
FOSSEUX	22	6.0 a.m	Company entrained at FOSSEUX for Roads and proceeded to BLAIRVILLE (Third Army) with 4 trade Brigade.	
BLAIRVILLE	23		Officers reconnoitred the Area.	
COURCELLES	24	5.50 am	Company paraded and proceeded to HAMELINCOURT to dig line of posts after look moved to COURCELLES where HQ and transport has moved in the meantime.	
	25	5 pm	Line of posts dug N. of COURCELLES to ADINFERVILLE and after work Company march back to DOUCHY to join HQ and transport. Company started 6.0 am.	
		6 pm	Company proceeded to COURCELLES to dig line of posts with instructions to hold the line on completion of work until relieved. On telph. Company marched to MONCHY when HQ and transport has moved in the meantime. Arrived at MONCHY at 6 am.	
MONCHY	26		Officers occupied all day reconnoitring Army Line with a view to digging at night.	
	27		Company left MONCHY at 5 pm to work on Army Line	

WAR DIARY or INTELLIGENCE SUMMARY

Army Form C. 2118.

Place	Date	Hour	Summary of Events and Information	Remarks and references to Appendices
	28		Canadians on journey to Front. Reached site of work 6 am. Resumed instructions from Lt. Col. 92nd Bn to assume command of 3 Field Coys and to 29 Coy. orders from MILEY WOOD to ADINFER WOOD and to assembly the 2nd Vyt. East of the infantry who were to attack by the "Blueway" during the night. Received orders at 5 am to withdraw 3 Field Coys to West side of ADINFER WOOD and await further instructions.	
	29		At 8.30 am order from 92nd Bde to occupy PURPLE LINE from LITTLE FARM to JUESNOY FARM and to hold the line at all costs. Transport moved to BIENVILLERS. Instructions to take Company to ADINFER WOOD and hold line in support to 11th EAST YORKS REGT in Gvd command of the 3 Field Coys. all wounded command of 2nd Field Coy. One Sapper wounded. Transport moved to POMMIER.	
	30		Company continued to hold the line. 1 Sapper wounded.	
	31		Company relieved by 219 Field Company and marches to SOUASTRE to join H.Q. and Transport.	

[signature]
Lt Henry Hope RE
Lt 2/Lt
OC 210 Fd Coy RE

A595

31st Divisional Engineers

210th FIELD COMPANY R.E. ::: APRIL 1918.

ORIGINAL.

CONFIDENTIAL.

WAR DIARY

of

210th Field Company.R.E.

From 1/4/18 to 30/4/18.

VOLUME XXVIII

WAR DIARY or INTELLIGENCE SUMMARY

Army Form C. 2118. Vol 28

Place	Date	Hour	Summary of Events and Information	Remarks and references to Appendices
SOUASTRE	1/4/18		Company marched from SOUASTRE to HALUZEL	
HALUZEL	2/4/18		Company proceeded by Bus to TINQUES and subsequently marched to CAUCORT	
CAUCORT	3/4/18 to 6/4/18		Training of Company and three days Rifle with Arms, fac Rite a	
HERMIN	8/4/18		Proceeded by march to HERMIN. O/C inspected site of Subsequent Coy. line with C.C. First Army. Lt. Gibson T.G. Jones the Coy. by Bus.	
	9/4/18		Company moved by lorry to HANQUETIN. Officers checking at work to capture nest of 1000 American Engineers during the afternoon and late	
HANQUETIN	10/4/18		Subsequent the work. Worked on Army Line. 2.30 pm. lorries & lies at Intlway are from work and billets at HANQUETIN. Reached Camp at 3.30 pm. and Company (less transport) proceeded by Bus at 4.45 pm. to TINQUES. Reporting to O/C. 3rd Colbelsream Guards on arrival. Coke buttered billets to Company Lines at TINQUES x Roads at 10.20 pm. Company proceeded to embussing point at 10.30 pm. & Busses arrived. Company spent the night alongside the road	
TINQUES	11/4/18		Busses arrived 12.15 pm. Company entrained and arrived at STRAZEELE Farm. Ordered by G.O.C. 4th Guards Bde. to billet at Heath Farm	

WAR DIARY
or
INTELLIGENCE SUMMARY.
(Erase heading not required.)

Army Form C. 2118.

Place	Date	Hour	Summary of Events and Information	Remarks and references to Appendices
STRAZEELE	12	4 am	Received Orders from 4 Infante Bde to move to VIEUX BERQUIN and report at 5 am and reported at 6 am. Company marched out at 4th Infante Bde H.Q. 6 am. Instructed to billet Company.	
		8 pm	Company employed digging fresh dug line. No.4 R Company carried up Ammunition and Rations. On finishing No.4 R Company proceeded to billets in BOIS D'AVAL arriving 11 am. Company posted along Northern edge of BOIS D'AVAL with instructions to hand approaches through the road.	
	13	4 pm	Instructions to 4 Infante Bde to be ready to move by Command at once in lighting order and report at Brigade H.Q. On shorting received information that the enemy has broken the line on the right and immediately to at once dig a series of posts in front of the Eastern edge of the BOIS D'AVAL and to occupy this line. The Bat. keep very heavy held the line in support Australian m.g fire and the vickers of the Line. In sullent to the Australian Machine Gunners who held a series of posts approximately 150ˣ in front.	

Army Form C. 2118.

WAR DIARY
or
INTELLIGENCE SUMMARY.
(Erase heading not required.)

Instructions regarding War Diaries and Intelligence Summaries are contained in F.S. Regs., Part II. and the Staff Manual respectively. Title pages will be prepared in manuscript.

Place	Date	Hour	Summary of Events and Information	Remarks and references to Appendices
BORRE	14	5am	Orders to withdraw from line and move to BORRE.	
	15		Company testing and training.	
	16			
	17		Company working on second zone defences.	
	18		Company moved to A SOUVERAIN.	
	19		Company working on 4 Franks Role Area hung of support line	
	20 to 27		Construction of Breastworks of sandbags. Preparation of Copy Work. Company moved to HONDEGHEM. New line being handed over to 510 Field Co. at 29 Divn.	
HONDEGHEM	28		Company training. Sites for Rifle & Lewis gun Rifle "C" and "D" Line Hazebrouck Defences.	
	29 to 30		Company working on or of 3 killed 6 OR wounded Casualties during month 3 killed 6 OR wounded	

H Henly
Major RE
OC 210 Feb 6 RE

ORIGINAL.

CONFIDENTIAL.

WAR DIARY
of
210th Field Company. R.E.
From 1/5/18 to 31/5/18.

VOLUME ~~XXVII~~
XXIX.

VOL 27

WAR DIARY
or
INTELLIGENCE SUMMARY
(Erase heading not required.)

Army Form C. 2118.

Place	Date	Hour	Summary of Events and Information	Remarks and references to Appendices
HONDEGHEM	1/5/18 to 9/5/18		Company working on HAZEBROUCK (Defences) Defence Lines C. D.	
	10/5/18 to 23/5/18		Company working on Second Zone Defences, Lines B & C and CAESTRE and THIEUSHOUK Defences.	
	23/5/18		Moved to BLARINGHEM. Relieved by 90th Field Co. R.E.	
	24/5/18 to 31/5/18		Company Rest and Training.	

J. Hern, Major R.E.
3rd Field Co. R.E.
OC 210

ORIGINAL.

CONFIDENTIAL.

WAR DIARY

of

210th Field Company. R.E.

From June 1st, 1918 to June 30th, 1918.

VOLUME ~~XXVIII~~ XXX

VOL 29

WAR DIARY
or
INTELLIGENCE SUMMARY
(Erase heading not required.)

Army Form C. 2118

Place	Date	Hour	Summary of Events and Information	Remarks and references to Appendices
BLARINGHEM	1/6/18		Company continued training on and between these dates.	
	"			
	14/6/18			
STAPLES	15/6/18		Company marches to STAPLES and engaged on have notice to	
	16/6/18		increase of enemy attack. Lieut R.J. O'RR detailed to return to	
				Base being officially Medically unfit
RACQUINGHEM	17/6/18		Company marches to RACQUINGHEM	
	18/6/18			
	"		Company continues training on and between these dates.	
	19/6/18			
HAZEBROUCK	20/6/18		Moves to forward area and relieves 497 Field Co. R.E. (29th Div)	
	21/6/18		Coy HQrs & packs billeted north of 223rd Field Co. R.E. Left Brigade area	
	22/6/18		Working parties on Railways and Rois Defences or	
	23/6/18		nothing on F. de Sec. Rois Defences, STAARTEN BROOCK Defences &	
	24/6/18		Two sections (Nos 1 & 2) performing to and fro Cattle gate engaged	
	26/6/18		in operations with Greeting of O/C 211 Field Co. R.E. The work	
	27/6/18		of these must section being the training and construction of posts	
	28/6/18		captured by the infantry at JOMBERT FARM and VERTE RUE	

Army Form C. 2118

WAR DIARY
or
INTELLIGENCE SUMMARY
(Erase heading not required.)

Instructions regarding War Diaries and Intelligence Summaries are contained in F. S. Regs., Part II. and the Staff Manual respectively. Title Pages will be prepared in manuscript.

Place	Date	Hour	Summary of Events and Information	Remarks and references to Appendices
	29/8/15		Lieut. H F A KEATING and Sapper JALODOIN killed and Sgt BROWN and Sapper JAFFERS PATEHURST and NEBBLETHWAITE wounded during these operations	
	30/8/15		Fort Cottages to Left Brigade Area. Erection of S.G. proof shelter - COBLEY COTTAGE - POOLEY FARM. Notch &	

J.B. Kenyon Major R.E.
1 Feb 16
O.C. 210 (?) Field Co. R.E.

[Stamp: 3 FIELD COMPANY ROYAL ENGINEERS]

1875 Wt. W593/826 1,000,000 4/15 J.B.C. & A. A.D.S.S./Forms/C. 2118.

ORIGINAL.

CONFIDENTIAL.

WAR DIARY

of

210th Field Company.R.E.

from 1/7/18 to 31/7/18.

VOLUME ~~XXXX~~ XXXI

VOL 31.

Army Form C. 2118

WAR DIARY
or
INTELLIGENCE SUMMARY
(Erase heading not required.)

Place	Date	Hour	Summary of Events and Information	Remarks and references to Appendices
AU SOUVERAIN	1/7/18 to 31/7/18		Company working in Left Brigade Area & the following work:- Corley Cottage - Volley Farm Sunset Cottages of Lavertz Shelter to Brigade H.Q. Construction of "Dry weather Track" and Bridges Improvements to 1 Line consisting of Duckboard Track, Trench Boards, Beaches of Elephant Shelters to Basket and Sandbag hut. P.M. and Tunnel.

J. Pemberton Major RE
OC 210 Field Coy RE | |

31/7/18

ORIGINAL.

CONFIDENTIAL.

WAR DIARY

of

210th Field Company.R.E.

From 1/8/18 to 31/8/18.

VOLUME XXXII

Army Form C. 2118

WAR DIARY
or
INTELLIGENCE SUMMARY
(Erase heading not required.)

Instructions regarding War Diaries and Intelligence Summaries are contained in F. S. Regs., Part II. and the Staff Manual respectively. Title Pages will be prepared in manuscript.

Place	Date	Hour	Summary of Events and Information	Remarks and references to Appendices
Au Souvrain	1/8/16 to 11/8/16		Company working on left Brigade area to improvement to Tramp Line of Advance. Section of Rathalow HQ, Repairs to Roads &c.	
Gd Hassard	11/8/16 to 22/8/16		Relieved by 211th Field Co RE and moves to Gd Hassard. Company is Reserve working on Section of Div Rails Roads, R.A. Post & period Back Area Post	
Le Peuplier	23/8/16		Moves to Le Peuplier and relieves 63rd Field Co RE (9 Divn) two Sections at HQ and two East of Coesfre. Company working on Gran Line of Advance, Section of Bn HQ and Back Area Post.	
Fletre	31/8/16		Company moves East of Fletre	

[stamp: FIELD COMPANY ROYAL ENGINEERS]

[signature]
1 Feb 16
OC 2nd [?] Field Co RE

ORIGINAL.

CONFIDENTIAL:

WAR DIARY

of

210th Field Company.R.E.

From 1st Sept. to 30th Sept. 1918.

VOLUME XXXI//

WAR DIARY or INTELLIGENCE SUMMARY

Army Form C. 2118

VOL 31

Instructions regarding War Diaries and Intelligence Summaries are contained in F.S. Regs., Part II. and the Staff Manual respectively. Title Pages will be prepared in manuscript.

(Erase heading not required.)

[210th Field Company Royal Engineers stamp, OCT 6]

Place	Date	Hour	Summary of Events and Information	Remarks and references to Appendices
BAILLEUL	1/9/18		Coy moved to 17.P.20.A. E/F/BAILLEUL to repair road and clear retired H.Qs.	
	2/9/18		Standing railway embankment two O.R. wounded by enemy shellfire.	
	3/9/18		Camp formed in O.17.c. and work continued as usual.	
	4/9/18		Coy moved forward to 7.25.a.02. Continuing work on road.	
	5/9/18		Coy moved back to P.27.e. bivouac under Adv. DHQ covered hours.	
	6/9/18		Coy working on DHQ water supply, road &c.	
	7/9/18			
	8/9/18			
	9/9/18			
	10/9/18		Major Joseph on leave to UK 30 days.	
CAESTRE	11/9/18		Coy moved to CAESTRE for work on crater quarries for DHQ CAESTRE.	
	12/9/18		Work on leave in CAESTRE for DHQ	
	to		No 3 Section surveyed road 6/9/18 & Wardrop Camp 7.25.a. for use and	
	21/9/18		Divisional Artillery.	
	22/9/18		Company moves 3rd section to 7.5.30. later one sent on NIEPPE SYSTEM.	
	23/9/18		Section 2 and 4 push divisional road work at PETIT MUNQUE FARM.	
	24/9/18		Coy working on laying plank road material, R.E.D. work and several Gas	
	to		curtains. Coy push in her 6.3	
	27/9/18			
	28/9/18		Section Standing by for further progress, prepare to move forward to big post on Nov 69	
	29/9/18		Section 2 moved forward to above and found further enemy cratered cratered at LA MOTTE	
	30/9/18		work on above. Bivouac under LA MOTTE Chateau Caves were also taken.	

[Signature]

ORIGINAL.

CONFIDENTIAL.

WAR DIARY

of

210th Field Company.R.E.

From 1/10/18 to 31/10/18.

VOLUME XXXIV

VOL 32

Army Form C. 2118

WAR DIARY
or
INTELLIGENCE SUMMARY
(Erase heading not required.)

Instructions regarding War Diaries and Intelligence Summaries are contained in F. S. Regs., Part II. and the Staff Manual respectively. Title Pages will be prepared in manuscript.

Place	Date	Hour	Summary of Events and Information	Remarks and references to Appendices
PLOEGSTEERT	1/10/18		Company working to forming ways in road. Note weekly construction of footbridge over Rive LYS for passage of Infantry	
WARNETON	16/10/18		Company moves to WARNETON and completed Pontoon Bridge	
	17/10/18		over Rive LYS including approaches and road LEAS	
CROIX BLANCHE	18/10/18		Company moves to CROIX BLANCHE	
TOURCOING	19/10/18		Company moves to TOURCOING	
	19/10/18		Nothing on construction of footbridge in HATTRELOS, repairs to roads to (Note: 92nd Inf Bde)	
LEERS-NORD	21/10/18		Company moves to LEERS-NORD	
	22/10/18		Company under orders to be ready to bridge the Rive L'ESCAUT	
	23/10/18		Company preparing trestles	
MOUSCRON	24/10/18		at PECQ preparing trestles Mouscron and Jones 9th Inf	
	25/10/18		proceeds to reach	
	26/10/18		Bde front STAEGHEM move to l'ESCAUT. Work on demolishing Pontoon Bridge	
STAEGHEM	27/10/18		move to Rive L'ESCAUT and preparing to Bfg my Rive	
VICHTE	30/10/18		over Rive L'ESCAUT to VICHTE	
	31/10/18		moves towards	

ORIGINAL.

CONFIDENTIAL.

WAR DIARY

of

210th Field Company. R.E.

From 1/11/18 to 30/11/18.

VOLUME ~~XXXIII~~ XXXV.

VOL. 33

Army Form C. 2118

WAR DIARY
or
INTELLIGENCE SUMMARY

(Erase heading not required.)

Instructions regarding War Diaries and Intelligence Summaries are contained in F.S. Regs., Part II. and the Staff Manual respectively. Title Pages will be prepared in manuscript.

Place	Date	Hour	Summary of Events and Information	Remarks and references to Appendices
VICHTE	1/11/18		Company returned to BISSEGHEM ready to proceed to bridging SCHELDT	
	2/11/18			
MOULIN	3/11/18		Company moved to MOULIN. Divers returned to the Rest Area	
	4/11/18		Company Equipment scheduled to assembly of pontoon traits	
	5/11/18		Company to COURTRAI and works in R.E. park in building of light Bridges	
COURTRAI	6/11/18			
	7/11/18			
	8/11/18		Front section moves to OOTEGHEM for bridging work at COUTHEM in case of advance	
OOTEGHEM	9/11/18		Company moves to OOTEGHEM and subsequently to RUGGE to light bridges construction over the River SCHELDT during the day	
ORROIR	10/11/18		Company marches to ORROIR	
RENAIX	11/11/18		Company moves to RENAIX. Without the Armature signed	
	12/11/18		Proceeds to try 92 Infantry Brigade at EVERBECQ. Orders cancelled & they March Company returns to RENAIX	
AVELGHEM	14/11/18		Company moves to AVELGHEM	

Army Form C. 2118

WAR DIARY
or
INTELLIGENCE SUMMARY
(Erase heading not required.)

Instructions regarding War Diaries and Intelligence Summaries are contained in F. S. Regs., Part II. and the Staff Manual respectively. Title Pages will be prepared in manuscript.

Place	Date	Hour	Summary of Events and Information	Remarks and references to Appendices
LAUWE	18/11/18		Company agreed to LAUWE and Bus Section during the period in January	
	23/11/18			
MENIN	24/11/18		Company marched to MENIN and found qrs. Infantry Bregade High.	
YPRES	25/11/18		Company marched to YPRES.	
STEENVOORDE	26/11/18		Company marched to STEENVOORDE.	
STAPLES	27/11/18		Company marched to STAPLES.	
LUDASSQUES	28/11/18		Company marched to LUDASSQUES.	
	29/11/18		Company refitting	
	30/11/18		Company refitting	

A McIntyre
Major RE
OC 210 Fld Coy RE

1875   Wt. W593/826   1,000,000   4/15   J.B.C. & A.   A.D.S.S./Forms/C. 2118.

ORIGINAL.

CONFIDENTIAL.

WAR DIARY

of

210th Field Company.R.E.

From 1/12/18 to 31/12/18.

VOLUME XXXIV

Vol 34

Army Form C. 2118

WAR DIARY or INTELLIGENCE SUMMARY

(Erase heading not required.)

Instructions regarding War Diaries and Intelligence Summaries are contained in F.S. Regs., Part II. and the Staff Manual respectively. Title Pages will be prepared in manuscript.

Place	Date	Hour	Summary of Events and Information	Remarks and references to Appendices
AUDRUICQ	1/12/15		Regt. A.S. Journey of Lt O'Brien	
ST. OMER	2/12/15		Company moved to Audruicq Camp for R.O.D. at St Omer. Nothing to record for in Camp	
"	3/12/15		Nothing to record. Working parties to Camp	
"	4/12/15		Church Parade	
"	5/12/15			
"	6/12/15		Training and Rehearsal of Government Parade	
"	7/12/15			
"	8/12/15		1 Section took Round of A R.E. 7 Met who had on bank of	
"	9/12/15		Ry. Canal to R.O.D. at St Omer	
"	10/12/15		2 Section in position in Camp	
"	11/12/15		2 Sections of numbers taken to work in Govt Camp at St Omer	
"	12/12/15		Church Parade	
"	13/12/15		1 Officer and 1 Section of Company working in Camp	
"	14/12/15		UMBERS	
"	15/12/15		2 sections to govt. Commence Push Labor of Hotel	
"	16/12/15		operated by R.O.D. Commenced Hutment + Boiler	
"	17/12/15		Company working in Camp + transport to Boiler	
"	18/12/15		and 075 + 130 to St Omer	

J. M---- Lieut
30.310 Feb C.R.E.
1/1/19

WAR DIARY.

of the

210th. FIELD COMPANY R.E.

for the month of JANUARY. 1919.

VOLUME 37.

Vol. 37

Army Form C. 2118

WAR DIARY
or
INTELLIGENCE SUMMARY
(Erase heading not required.)

Instructions regarding War Diaries and Intelligence Summaries are contained in F.S. Regs., Part II. and the Staff Manual respectively. Title Pages will be prepared in manuscript.

Place	Date	Hour	Summary of Events and Information	Remarks and references to Appendices
ST OMER	1/1/19 to 31/1/19		Company billetted in between late No 10 Stationary Hospital and working on improvement to camps occupied by units of the Divison. & Shade jobs in the Area. Demobilisation continued during the month.	4/2/19 [signature] Lt OC 210 Field Co RE

WAR DIARY.

210th FIELD COMPANY, ROYAL ENGINEERS.

FEBRUARY, 1919.

VOL 38

Army Form C. 2118

WAR DIARY

INTELLIGENCE SUMMARY

(Erase heading not required.)

Instructions regarding War Diaries and Intelligence Summaries are contained in F. S. Regs., Part II. and the Staff Manual respectively. Title Pages will be prepared in manuscript.

Place	Date	Hour	Summary of Events and Information	Remarks and references to Appendices
ST OMER.	12/7/19 to 13/7/19		Company billetted in previous huts. No. 10 Stationary Hospital in January. Works parties out — improvements as minor repairs in the neighbourhood.	
-do-	14/7/19		Owing to reduction in strength due to demobilization, company moved into huts and occupied by 223 Field Coy. R.E.	
-do-	15/7/19 to 28/7/19.		Company remained in the above camp. Small jobs carried out as required in the neighbourhood. Several water pipe bursts due to frost were attended to during the latter part of the month. Demobilization continued up to the 20th of the month. Strength of the company was down to later '73' — including a number of men on leave for reduction to the Army of Occupation	

[signature] Lieut
[signature] RE

1875 Wt. W593/826 1,000,000 4/15 J.B.C. & A. A.D.S.S./Forms/C. 2118.

Army Form C. 2118

WAR DIARY
or
INTELLIGENCE SUMMARY

(Erase heading not required.)

210th Field Coy. R.E.

No. 37

Instructions regarding War Diaries and Intelligence Summaries are contained in F.S. Regs, Part II. and the Staff Manual respectively. Title Pages will be prepared in manuscript.

Place	Date	Hour	Summary of Events and Information	Remarks and references to Appendices
ST. OMER	1-3-19 to 31-3-19		The company remained in the hutted camp, with the 211th and 223rd Field Coys during February. Work consisted of small repairs and improvements to various camps in the neighbourhood. The company being warned to cadre strength, demobilization began. As is possible the cadre was made up of released men; those left for retention in the Army of Occupation being taken off the same unit. A few officers	Off
	6-3-19		Major D.E. STEIBELT M.C. handed over command of the company to Capt. C.S.T. JONES and left for England on 9-3-19 for demobilization.	Off
	26-3-19 27-3-19		The company vehicles with the exception of G.S. wagons & men went out to WIZERNES where they were parked near the railway station ready for loading on train on definition of the cadre	Off
	31-3-19	22.00 hrs	The number of animals in possession of the company was reduced to 2 mules. Order was received to despatch returnable men for the Army of Occupation on the morning of 1-4-19 to report to O.C. 62nd (Highland) Div. & that Cadre detailed to hold the coy to proceed to ANTWERP to join R.E. Works Coy.	Off

C.S. Jones
Capt.
O.C. 210 Field Coy. R.E.

210TH FIELD COMPANY
APR 1/19
ROYAL ENGINEERS

Army Form C. 2118.

WAR DIARY 210th F.C., R.E.

INTELLIGENCE SUMMARY

(Erase heading not required.)

Instructions regarding War Diaries and Intelligence Summaries are contained in F.S. Regs., Part II. and the Staff Manual respectively. Title Pages will be prepared in manuscript.

Place	Date	Hour	Summary of Events and Information	Remarks and references to Appendices
ST. OMER	1-4-19 to 30-4-19		The cadre of the 210th F.C. Coy R.E. remained at St. Omer awaiting orders to entrain and to proceed to England. The wagons were kept at WIZERNES station, when entraining was expected to take place. A guard —lies at WIZERNES in charge of the wagons. Up to the end of the month no orders to entrain had been received. Meanwhile small jobs, as required by neighbouring units, were carried out when occasion arose.	

J. Doun, Capt.
O.C. 210 F.C. R.E.

www.ingramcontent.com/pod-product-compliance
Lightning Source LLC
Chambersburg PA
CBHW081436160426
43193CB00013B/2300